SONNETS
TWO TEN

SONNETS
TWO TEN

A Book of Sonnets

Peter Thorpe

To order additional copies of this book, contact:
Xlibris Corporation
1-888-795-4274
www.Xlibris.com
Orders@Xlibris.com
15718-THOR

CONTENTS

To my dearest Nathalie, who made this book possible.

LIFE OF A TOY

I watch the Slinky toy descending stairs,
A nude and awkward spring that flips its weight
Forward and down again: it seldom cares
Who's watching it. It never can be late

Because it lives outside of time. It never
Begins or ends, as far as it's concerned;
It never loves or dies or lives forever
And can't forget the things it never learned.

Some times I wish I were a Slinky toy,
Lurching through life without a heart or brain;
I'd have no thoughts or memories to annoy
My steely soul; I'd have no hope, no pain.

I'd simply step, with this ungainly stride,
Over the precipice, so deep and wide.

SENIOR CITIZEN AT THE
PIANO BAR

Please play that song again, but please don't say
The title; let me see if I can guess:
It has to do with love, I think, unless
It has to do with hats and papier-maché

And things of little substance. Damn me now,
That title quite escapes me! Play it again,
If you don't mind, and I'll consult the men
I used to be. Miss, you can take a bow

When you get done, and maybe I'll leave a five
In that big whiskey glass. I love your fingers,
The way they lithely writhe, the way they dive
In ventricles of my brain where memory lingers

Briefly before it slips away and cools
In caves of age where love just sits and drools.

THE WRONG WOMAN

Proceeded to read some verse by Maxine Kumin,
By Sharon Olds, Mark Strand, and Rita Dove.
Proceeded to fall in love with the wrong woman:
She's married, much too young, and not in love

With me. If I had half a brain and strength
To keep away from her, that's what I'd do.
Proceeded to break my rules and ran the length
Of a football field and shouted out, "Yoo-hoo!

Please wait and walk with me, you lovely girl;
We'll stroll around the lake a couple of times;
We'll talk of poets and the way they hurl
Their bones against the wind with clumsy rhymes."

Proceeded to bore her with my rusty chat;
She smiled and walked away, and that was that.

OLD GUY AT SCOTT CARPENTER POOL

July: the smell of chlorine by the pool,
Odors of suntan lotions on the thighs
Of women still in high school, and the cool
Expressions on the faces of the guys.

What am I doing here, a senior wag,
Whose pallid pectorals have turned to dough,
Whose skin hangs like a milky plastic bag
With tattoos from a couple of wars ago?

The James Dean lifeguard gives me quizzical looks:
I don't belong; I came here to molest,
He thinks. I think he's wrong. I brought some books
(Faulkner and Nabokov); I'll read the best.

I'll smear zinc oxide on my lower lip,
And if my memory calls me, take a dip.

LOVE AND BANKERS' HOURS

A penny saved? Why, that's a penny earned
—Unless you're talking hearts and lips and flowers,
Sweet somethings and the way my passions burned
When I first saw her ankles. Banker's hours

Are something lovers never keep; their work
Is never done because it never begins
Until they break apart and start to shirk
The duties of their thighs and knees and shins.

Ah, then they're never lovers any longer,
Forfeiting all the manias of the name;
Oh, then they get more serious and much stronger
As down they drop where everything's the same

—And dull, and dull, and love is just a flea,
Sinking somewhere a thousand miles at sea.

LOVERS' PICNIC

What shall we do today, my love? Shall we
Go swimming at the "Y," or shall we hike
Over the underpass down by the tree
That roots itself so deep? What would you like?

Have you eaten yet? I have a bottle of red,
Some sandwiches, a couple o' Milky Ways,
And one fresh ear of corn. Come, let us spread
Our blanket on the grass that briefly stays

And feast ourselves before it starts to rain.
Timing is everything, some Russian said,
The day before he died in horrible pain,
Twisting and turning there on the drenched bed.

So set the basket down, and let's get on:
Timing is all we have when we are gone.

CHET BURIES THE AFFAIR

We spend a lot of time together now:
Some folks begin to talk but most do not;
Some neighbors saw us kiss and noticed how
There was some passion there, but not a lot.

Some folks (a few) may wonder where we're headed
And whether we think we'll rise above despair
Some sultry months from now when we have bedded
For the last time, burying the affair.

I wish you well. I hope that you an Lou
Get back together; you had something there
That still could work. You grew some dahlias too
That Lou was fond of, and he liked your hair.

I think we'll end this. I will move away
To Boston maybe, or perhaps L.A.

GENERAL WASHINGTON

Maximum George, they call me Maximum George,
    The ones who won by surging over the line
    In many a gouging fight —at Valley Forge,
And all the red and gurgling fields. They're mine.

    I did not buy the name of Maximum G.;
    They bought it for me, officers and men
    Who quick-stepped into serial war with me
And came out dead or old. And now and then

    When I look back, here at the century's end,
    I see their faces, every one. I hear them
    Saying sometimes, "The war will never mend
The things that it was meant to, and we fear them,

    The wars to come, we mean, and how we'll fight
For Maximum George, the strangler of the night."

HOUSE OF LOGS

With Lincoln Logs I build a suitable house,
With dark green plastic chimney and a stoop,
Veranda-like, a doorway that a mouse
Might stumble through, a metal outside hoop

Where rats might shoot some baskets, and some grass
Made out of Christmas paper for the lawn.
The Lincoln Logs are brownish, like old brass
That's been allowed to tarnish on and on,

The way our marriage did. We built our home
Way back in 'eighty-one, before those fogs
Blinded our souls and we began to roam,
And everything fell. I build with Lincoln Logs

Today and nothing else, for safety's sake;
Let them collapse; what difference does it make?

BY THE NOSE

I like it when you lead me by the nose
Through all the village streets, a length of rope
About my neck, your purple pantyhose
Around my waist. They tell me I'm your dope,

And they are right. You make me wear a dress,
A saffron dress, though I'm a six-foot man
And burly as a redwood tree (I guess).
Here's what you said (I listen to my Nan):

"Manhood which has to prove itself is not
Real manhood, dear; it proves itself by showing
Tulips and daffodils and streaks of snot
That mothers wipe away and then by blowing,

For free, the noses of the small and weak.
When you've done that you will have climbed the peak."

JUST WALKING

Just walking you can work up quite a sweat,
Especially if you walk across your mind;
It takes forever, and you're apt to get
Fatigued and winded; then you'll fall behind,

Without quite knowing, Nan, what lies ahead.
No one can walk across my mind but me,
Or so you told me when we were in bed,
And then you walked across my Caspian Sea,

Staying afloat until you reached the shore.
You waved at me and shouted out some words
I could not hear. I heard the breakers roar;
I heard the ancient shriekings of the birds,

And all the energies of the bounding main.
Lovely to see you walk across my brain!

POEM ON HIS BIRTHDAY

Today's my birthday, Nan; I'm sixty-eight,
Still young enough to drive a car (I think)
But old enough to know that I'm —oh, wait,
Forgot what I was going to say. Let's drink,

In any case, an existential toast
To rolling stones uphill when there's no hill,
To fear and trembling when we have the most
To feel secure about, to strength of will

When will is mere idea; and, let me see,
What else? This hurts. You know my gnarly limbs
Don't work so well these days, and I can pee
Only with difficulty now. The flashlight dims

That used to light my brain. But I'm not through,
As long as I have laughter, Nan, and you.

IN KALAMAZOO

I feel that I've accomplished quite a lot
In this, my life, my long obstreperous trail,
By trying to be the things that I am not
And failing most of the time. I've chased a grail

Or two, and had one by the handle once,
But it slipped away. You know, the gal I had
In Kalamazoo, she slipped away. The (what?)
I didn't achieve, they helped me know a fad

From steady things with depth, and how our reach
Exceeds our rasp when we are growing hoarse
From giving advice to those we would impeach.
I wanted to be the President, of course,

And only became an air-raid warden, Nan,
In Kalamazoo. I hope I'm still your man.

HIGH MUCKY-MUCKS

High mucky-mucks and bigwigs call my shots
Whenever I ask them to; whenever I drop
My self-respect I sleep on army cots
Instead of mattresses, or down I plop

On some green park bench with the evening news
Over my face. Please wake me just at six
And tell me if it's Sunday; where's my booze?
My days become a game of pick-up-sticks

Whenever I drop my guard; my willpower slides
Down some dark rusty chute to where my reason
Cannot be found, and there my frivolous sides
Begin to shake with laughter out of season.

Sleeping so soundly on a poverty-cot:
This is a serious business, is it not?

PANTIES, GARTER BELTS, AND BRASSIERES

Half-naked ladies staff my Saturday dreams
When I have gone to bed with numerous drinks;
The women, they are middle-aged, it seems,
And buxom too, and dressed in greens and pinks,

Except to say that some are bare from waist
To face, with breasts as full as cantaloupes,
And some are bare to toe and all unlaced,
So as to show the slumbering man the hopes

That he can seldom entertain. This flesh,
It spills all over my dreams and in my face,
As these pneumatic women dance and mesh
Their lips and limbs with mine. There is no place

For this when I awake, I'm well aware,
And yet I'm glad I got to touch your hair.

THE GYROSCOPIC HUSBAND

My Nan, she fashions me, and I stay put
Whenever she goes away. I pay no mind
To other girls, no matter how the foot
Of bodily lust may prod me from behind.

I'm like the compass-card in steel-gray ships,
With lines and numbers that can point the way
No matter how the navy rolls and dips,
No matter how those women's bodies sway.

While everything around me moves, I rest,
Steady for Nan, as though I were in gimbals
Which let the compass ride and do its best
While house-high waves are crashing like the cymbals

In some Wagnerian theme. I just point north
As long as love is kind and sallying forth.

A FOOTBALL PLAYER KNOCKED

A football player knocked upon my door
This morning, Nan, in sweaty full regalia;
I hadn't seen this uniform before;
His helmet was the color of an azalea,

And all the rest was dull funereal black.
This player, he was not especially tall
Or wide or thick; he was a quarterback,
I guess; he held a scuffy-looking ball

Under his arm. I asked him what he wanted
And why he called on me on Monday morning.
He said he came to say my house was haunted
By windy fools. He wished to give me warning

Concerning insight, foresight, hindsight, Nan,
And how we keep the future in the can.

ERECTOR SET

I had an Erector Set when I was ten,
With narrow metal girders and some screws
And nuts, to hold together what was then
An emblem of the greatness I would choose

In later life —or so I thought. I built
A cart, a bridge, and also a little tower
Of shiny steel that wasn't supposed to tilt
But did. I even built an ungainly flower

With bolted stalk and petals made of steel.
I showed it to my father, who was polite
And told me he was late. Why do I feel
The cut of all his words, even tonight,

In darkest San Francisco, though I'm old
And my Erector Sets are made of gold?

EASTER POEM

Easter's for rising, Nan, not just for Jesus,
But all of us who seek to find our way;
Easter's a time for finding things that please us
Under the grass-stained eggs; why wait for May?

I found a chocolate rabbit: he was hollow
And smirking some; I bit off his right ear
And then the left: if I were asked to follow
This wounded rabbit for the rest of the year

I do not think I would. I will, however,
Follow my Nan till Jesus tells me not to,
And when he does I mean to part forever
With all the things that she is not. I've got to.

My Nan is with me till the cosmos falls
And Jesus (look who's talking) decks the halls.

THE DRAWBRIDGE

I let my drawbridge down today, to see
If anybody needed what I had;
I thought, "If no one comes to visit me,
I'll feel neglected and a little sad."

But then I thought, "So what, if no one comes?
It's pleasant in my castle all alone,
Counting my money on my toes and thumbs,
To pass this day, with an occasional moan

From dungeons under the floor." A drawbridge serves
To get acquainted or to get away
From anything in the land, if you have nerves
Of steel and can ignore the fray

You sometimes hear outside your stone redoubt.
Why let them in when you can shut them out?

PIE-FACE

Here's a suggestion, Nan: just take a pie,
A rich banana cream one, and then throw it
In my dull face. Don't hit a passer-by,
And please don't hit the President; he'll show it

Most likely to his girlfriends, and he'll eat it
Tonight and give a speech. So hit me square
Between the eyes, if possible; I need it
To stand my ego down and keep my hair

From parting in the middle like the sea
That Moses cut in two. My crusty pride,
It brags and struts and gets the best of me
—Unless my viable Nan can stem the tide

That's jumping in my veins, like some old question,
Which is the same, you see, as this suggestion.

FATHER'S DAY

Try counting backwards from one hundred, Dad,
By threes and then by fours and then by sevens,
And if you have some trouble and have had
An excess of time to answer, then the heavens

Are getting ready to receive you home,
Not right away perhaps, but down the road
Some miles through mist and fog. This poem,
I showed it to you yesterday and showed

It once again this morning, and you read it
So haltingly, as though it was a song
You'd never seen. You stumble and you edit
Everything that you see and get it wrong.

You hardly know me, Dad. It's me, your son!
Is the war over now, and have you won?

SUPERSONIC AIRLINER DOWN

You interrupted me to say it crashed,
The Concorde supersonic plane, in France,
Right after take-off, with all bodies smashed
Like drunken grapes in some old hideous dance.

It didn't strike a river or a town
—Only a restaurant whose unfinished diners
Shared death with all the travelers who went down
To share the final supper. Sad headliners

Who didn't choose this kind of grisly fame,
They never made it home this lovely day
But rather went to bed in bags, while flame
Still licked about the wreckage. We don't pray

As often as we should, nor can we die
The way we'd like to, lighting up the sky.

NAKED BOY

There was a boy who took his clothes off, Nan,
And stood alone in the middle of the street,
Waiting for cars to come: a full-grown man
Is what he did not want to be. His feet

Remained so firmly planted all day long,
But no cars came, and nobody walked the walk
That ran beside the grass; there was no song
From bird or beast or human being. I'll talk

Only a little more about this thing,
This fatalistic boy who was alone,
And then I'll drop it. I would rather sing
Of positivistic things, of muscle and bone

And mind and soul that seek to stay afloat
By treading water in the dungeon's moat.

THE BORING ONES

Hey Nan, come have a look! I've got a bike
And I can ride it with no hands; I own
A brand-new skateboard here, and if you'd like,
I'll show you stunts that I have never shown

To any other girl. What's that you say?
Don't bother, 'cause you've seen them all before?
Am I no hero now? Is there no way
To make the right impression? I'm a bore?

The thing about the bores is that they know
They're boring; they're just choosing not to face it;
They're lonesome as a pine that's covered with snow;
They've got a brain untied and just won't lace it.

—Easier just to wink and just pretend
The one who's smiling at you is your friend.

I BROKE YOUR STRING OF BEADS

I broke your string of beads last night,
Down in the kitchen, Nan, when all I wanted
Was just to say a prayer. All right, all right,
I wasn't going to pray; the house is haunted,

And I was going to chase the ghosts away
Through hexes and the like, twirling the beads;
But they ran in all directions. Who's to say
They'll ever all be found? Look in the weeds

To find a grain of salt, or in the straw
For the proverbial needle; shoot a dove
That flies at fifteen thousand feet: the law
Is always the same: the ones who fall in love,

And stay, have done the impossible, it seems,
In finding all the beads that make their dreams.

THE BAD FRIEND

I'll have the baked Alaska; that sounds good,
And maybe a cup of coffee with no cream.
Dinner with friends: the kind of thing that should
Go well, so when it doesn't it can seem

As though the chair's been pulled from under you
And you are dumped; and ten years later in life
The thing still smarts because it was too true
And false, that crack you made about my wife.

I have a plan: let's take a meal together
Just one more time. I'll meet you down at Denny's
On Monday morning, regardless of the weather;
We'll use the senior menu and save pennies.

Then you can tell me how and where you've been
And why the blood comes dribbling down your chin.

THE GOOD-LUCK MAN

I nailed a horseshoe, Nan, above my door,
To bring me luck; I bought a rabbit's foot
  To finger in my pocket at the store
Where luck is sold; I smeared a little soot

  Above my eyes and cut a switch of birch
To keep the selfish geese away from me;
  I said a prayer but did not get to church
And could not seem to change the "I" to "We."

Back to the drawing board I've gone, dear Nan,
  A hundred times or more, to fix all that,
  To find a name and smash a coffee can
With ball-peen hammers, see, until it's flat.

  I go in search of all the fates that fit me;
With any luck, I'll never know what hit me.

LOCAL TELEVISION NEWS

I watch the anchorman on local news,
With fifty-dollar haircut and a smile
He rents from somewhere —he will keep the booze
Off-camera. Next to him, in boomer style,

The anchorwoman sits, perky and cute,
Talking about a car wreck down on Main,
Three dead, ooo, that's too bad. I touch the "mute"
And watch her wet lips pull stuff from her brain,

Wondering what those lips might do at home.
The anchorman, it's his turn now; he's silent
Just like the perky one, who pulls a comb
Through her blonde hair. And now the news is violent:

A prominent anchorwoman has been shot,
And all the anchor men —well, they've been bought.

MY TOWER OF VOWELS

My silo full of sounds, my tower of vowels:
That's where I keep my keepers, I mean poems
Or parts of poems I find behind my jowls
And knapsack brain, the ones that have no homes

As yet in any work that I would show,
But yet the ones that have some drosslessness
In my strict tower of vowels. Poems tell me no
More often than they don't, and I confess,

The chaff I find too often in my silo
Has seeped outside, like oil or tar or gas.
Let's sleep on these. The Venus (stump) de Milo
Was made I guess by going to a class

Where patience and adrenalin were taught,
And what was durable and what was not.

LA JOLLA COVE

I played some volleyball upon the beach
Early today, beside La Jolla Cove;
One of the female players had a reach
That went beyond the net; her body drove

Itself like some machine made by a saint
Or else a devil; this was heaven and hell
With thighs and breasts and face I wanted to paint,
Though I was not a painter. I played well

But never well enough to catch her eye
Beside La Jolla Cove. A baby seal
Was rolling in the sand nearby, the sky
Was hazy, and I thought I heard the wheel

Of Fortune turning high above my head.
And my old legs, my God, they felt like lead.

VALENTINE FOR NAN

Too many Valentines are like dull ships
That clumsily put to sea and sail and sail,
To get to what they think they want —some lips?
A wishing well? Free rides? Too often they fail,

Or chicken out, or sink, or just get lost
Among the crowds of would-be lover-boys
Who buy those drugstore Valentines embossed
With someone else's sentiments and joys.

The Valentines I send you, Nan, are real
And from my own particular fleet of thoughts
And feelings, stout container ships that deal
In what will glow: I send forget-me-nots,

Sweet posies, tulips, daffodils, and all
My love, dear Nathalie, my bird, my doll.

YOU TOOK YOUR TIME

You took your time this time, redoubtable Nan;
My God, I thought you'd never get here, love;
Yet here you are beneath our old slow fan
That, Casablanca-like, goes round above

Our tousled heads as we rehearse our joys.
And here you are beneath my ignorant chest,
As we go round and round, like girls and boys
Too old, too young, to be here, but the best

At doing what we do this summer's day.
The Casablanca fan, it hums some hymns
And makes a breeze on San Francisco Bay;
We sail and haul and steer this with our limbs,

Whatever it is, whatever it wants to be
—A mule, a mouse, some candy, or a tree.

EIGHTY-YEAR-OLD MOVIE STAR

I heard the women talking on the bus:
"I hear he's eighty now," one of them said;
I think the women spoke for most of us
Long-in-the-tooth old lovers: straight ahead

Lies eighty in the road like some old tree,
Leaning and rotten long before it fell.
"The old dry stud is eighty," says the sea,
"And time goes slow and yet it goes pell-mell."

"The handsome ass-hound's eighty," says the land,
"And not so handsome anymore." He'll leave
Behind him what he fashioned with his hand
(Some clumsy paintings) and a kid, I believe,

As well as clumsy movies and a flair
For chasing boobs. Hey look! That's quite a pair!

TOKYO ROSE AND AXIS SALLY

Tokyo Rose and Axis Sally smiled
For the photographers down in the street,
And then they went to lunch. They talked and whiled
The day away, one tall and one petite.

And though they'd never met, they hit it off
As easily as a mortar shell might fall
In some unlucky foxhole, see, and doff
A couple of Yankee heads. Do you recall

The Banzai-Nazi war? Or are you young?
And when the prostitutes got out of jail,
Do you recall the ditties that were sung?
And did they have the morals of a snail,

With shiny slime and with no rhyme or reason?
And who of us has never thought of treason?

A SNAKE, BY DEFINITION

A snake, by definition, is a pit
In every stomach when we have no knowledge
That something's coming, Nan. You said, "Oh shit!
I'd never heard you swear before: in college

You were a perfect lady, and today
You're most unladylike, with Biblical reason:
I didn't see him either; he must play
A sly insidious game in many a season

In order to survive, and if we're scared
Or startled by the sudden stranger, Nan,
The fear that fastens on us we have shared
With most of nature's world since time began.

The thing that sneaks and takes us by surprise:
It means to murder us to make us wise.

SIR FRANCIS THE SEAGULL

Didja hear about Sir Francis? He got sucked,
Before he had a chance to dodge or dive,
Into a big jet intake. He got plucked
Quicker than any fowl that's now alive!

Came out in bits and pieces nicely fried,
Sir Francis did. His ending was absurd,
And yet what ending isn't? Like the tide,
He came and went. He got tagged out at third.

He lived to be the ripe old age of three
And hung around the airports of L.A.
He tried to get his sustenance for free
Near glide-paths of the jumbo jets. One day

—But it's too crude to tell. Just tip your hat
Or tip it not, and let it go at that.

WHEN WE HAVE SEEN A LOT

When we have seen a lot, when we have seen
The sun break right in two and then return
To what it was before it was a bean
In some primordial giant's storage urn,

When we have seen dogs fall in love with cats,
The pirate perched upon the giant's shoulder,
A Punch and Judy show that has no spats,
A planet that can spin and grow no older:

When we have seen all this, my dearest Nan,
What will we know, and will we know no more
Than when we started out? You have a fan
With which you cool your face when I'm a bore,

Waving it back and forth as on I write,
For all the live-long day and half the night.

SOLDIER OF ANCIENT TOWERS

I had a Sabine woman in my arms
But put her down and let her run away
Before the horrible weaponry that harms
The permanent soul could strike and have its say.

She shrieked (and who could blame her?) as she ran,
Her gold hair flying and her gown all torn;
The scratches on her arms and legs began
To bleed a little as I heard the horn

That once again was signaling retreat.
The Sabine women, they were safe for now;
The Sabine women with their tiny feet
Were running for the woods. I took a vow

To come another day and seek their knees
And do a soldier's business under the trees.

A HORROR MOVIE

That graphic music in the movie "Psycho,"
When son as mother stabs poor Janet Leigh:
Not all the insurance offered up by Geico
Could save that woman —no, nor you, nor me.

The music and the "ch, ch, ch" of the knife:
They're with me still today, though forty years
Have stooped me some and given me a wife
I didn't start with. Hair grows in my ears

And coffins yawn at me and seem to laugh,
As if to say that Hitchcock told the truth
In showing death the trickster as one half
Of all the lives we lead, from sniveling youth

To waxy age. Did Janet marry a hunk,
And who was cowering in that muddy trunk?

CHINESE CHECKERS

Don't poke your nose into my business, Nan,
  Unless you mean to stay a while and play
Some games of Chinese checkers with this man
  Who's sitting here and writing this today.

  Or maybe we could play a round or so
Of pick-up-sticks and then some blind-man's bluff,
  Followed by all the other games we know,
  Until we get fatigued and say, "Enough!"

  I need to go downtown. When I get back
We'll talk about the games we failed to play;
  The love we have is based upon the knack
  Of playing not and staying out of the way

  Of all those dusty demons in our heads,
The ones that move the monsters under our beds.

MORE ON GEORGE
WASHINGTON

George Obelisk, he stood tall among God's creatures;
Even in stocking feet he reached the sky;
He had a putty face with militant features,
And tense of mouth was he, about to cry

The battle cry, like a man of 'Seventy-Six.
He never changed expression, even in rain
That beat all day against his slabs and bricks
And ran on down his sides. His orchard brain

Was moving, growing, though we could not tell
At first. We had to listen for a while
Before we caught his constitutional drift
And came to see that Obelisk had style.

He had some art that doesn't look like art
And quietly chops in brain and groin and heart.

TEN-PENNY NAILS

I have a nail that can't be driven in,
Ten-penny nail that can't be hammered down,
Although it's sharp and hard as any sin,
Although the wood is soft as this whole town.

Some say my nail gets bent and I must wait
To get it out again and hammer it flat
Upon the basement floor, to make it straight,
As though it were a brand-new thing. The cat

Is frightened by the hammering in the house
And all my angry words that go along;
She scurries behind the furnace like a mouse
Running from whiskered foe. I sing my song:

God damn this nail that can't be hammered right.
God damn this house. God damn this star-lit night.

FROM QUEEN ANNE HILL

From Queen Anne Hill I'm watching Puget Sound
On a windy day. The whitecaps move as though
Harassed by —hold it, I don't want to found
Some metaphor and say "I told you so,"

As if I were the one who knew the forces
Better than all. Out there a lazy freighter
Is heading north. The captain took some courses,
I guess, in how to steer and how to cater

To nature's quick delinquent moods. And yet,
Even if he's a calm deliberate man,
The seas will have a surprise or two, I'll bet,
In store for him before he makes Japan.

Odds are he'll do just fine. The seagulls whirl
Like white and windblown skirts on some young girl.

THE JERK IS BACK FROM VEGAS

Hi Hon, it's me, your big chrome-plated daddy,
Just back from Vegas with a thousand bucks
They gave me for my seventy-seven Caddy
At Honest John's Used Cars. Las Vegas sucks

My pock-marked pockets dry and turns my wallet
Into a dead sow's ear, but I can't learn.
I guess I have that god-damned watchamacallit
Disease —you know, the one in which you burn

Money as though it's falling out of style,
As though there's no today and no tonight.
Where are you, Hon? Let's sit and drink a while:
I'll be here in the kitchen with the light

Turned off, and I'll be clever, quote unquote.
Where are you, dear? Jesus, what's this, a note?

BE GENIAL

Someone, I can't remember who, once said,
"Be genial all your life and you will reap
The scowls and frowns of those with brains of lead,
The ones who sojourn darkly under the heap

Of lemons that have fallen from the tree."
Someone, I can't remember who, declared,
"Be difficult all your life and you will see
More stars and sunshine than you are prepared

To witness or than you deserve. Remember:
The ones who seem so serious in their name
Are the least serious, and the glowing ember
Glows only to pretend it's still a flame."

You won't remember now who told you this
Or whether it's true at all. How about a kiss?

FINGERS

My thumbs and index fingers serve me well:
Being opposed, they help me grasp a wide
Variety, dear Nan: a stone, a bell,
A needle or a pencil or the hide

Of some illiterate mouse that comes to visit
Our winsome home just as the trap is set.
My index fingers and my thumbs —what is it?
Why are you interrupting me, my pet?

I know, I know, I'm boring you again,
Droning away on obvious facts and fictions,
The things you know as well as you know rain
And injury and sorrow —all the afflictions

That stick to us like well-chewed Wrigley's gum
Between the index finger and the thumb.

DEAD TEACHERS

Miss Palm, the English teacher, quit today,
Or was it yesterday, and Mr.Glass,
The mathematics teacher, faded away
Into the mists of Alz., before the class

Dismissed him as a teacher. Fat Miss Giles
Is teaching still and shows no signs of slowing,
Although she's slow. She paces in the aisles,
Like an awkward boat some imbecile is rowing.

I'll be a teacher someday too, I'm sure,
Raking the blackboard with my fingernails
And speaking with an alcoholic slur
Of shoes and ships and Kiwi wax and jails.

We lost three teachers but they're still around,
Walking like vegetables above the ground.

THESE BRIGHT STRING BEANS

These bright string beans upon the kitchen table
Lie in a heap, like soldiers who fought hard
And died for causes that they were unable
To fathom. Now there's no one to stand guard

Over these fallen dupes, so let me try
To monument them now with some kind words.
I'll place one bean to make the letter "I"
And place two here to make an "L." No birds

Will sing of this, I know, but I'll proceed
Until I've spelled the message out in green.
I'm green myself in this, and I will need
Your help and God's and that of every bean

Here on the kitchen table by the knife,
In this, the stinking crisis of my life.

STEP TEST

I took the step test once, in Fogarty's gym:
　You step up on a bench and then step down
And then step up again. It's dumb and all but grim,
　With beeper keeping time and Fogarty's frown

As he stands watching you, with big arms crossed.
　After five minutes of stepping hard and feeling
That both your lunch and breakfast will be lost,
You know just what you're made of; you are reeling

And queasy with fatigue. And then it stops
　And you sit down. Old Fogarty looks at you
And says you flunked the test; he calls the cops;
　They come and take you down where all is blue.

Blue in the face I was when my heart stopped
In Fogarty's gym. And I was stiffly propped.

TROUBLE WALKING

Staggering walk, I've got a staggering walk,
Just like James Cagney when he's had a blow,
Stumbling along with legs apart and awk-
Ward gesturing with the hands. I'll never know

Just how I got this way; the doctor said
It's water on the brain; my former wives
Said too much wrath and rage had bent my head,
And you, dear Nan, said those were former lives

And shouldn't be listened to. You said the only
Three things that matter now are you and I
And what the future holds. We won't be lonely,
You said, as long as Cagney's in the sky,

Smiling upon us from the crowds of stars
And helping us to find our getaway cars.

OUR WALL

Sought-after invitations I don't get:
I'm a low-lane, not a fast-lane, kind of guy;
The beautiful people climb aboard their jet,
But will they wave to us as they go by?

Say tell me, Nan, what year was that we went
To England with the teachers and bought tweeds;
And did we shop in Soho or in Kent,
And did we meet our deadlines and our needs?

Sought-after invitations you can win
By sending in your fingerprints, your soul,
And all the things you fought for in the war
Until there's nothing left, only a hole

Where other holes have been, and where the wall
We built today will keep us out. That's all.

SENIOR CITIZEN DRIVING AT NIGHT

The tractor-trailer rig that carries the cars,
Ten at a time, and fast, has Fords tonight,
Jiggling along at sixty under the stars
On a crowded Interstate Five. We're packed in tight

Just south of Bakersfield; it's hot; I'm wishing
To pass, but I'm afraid to swerve; my eyes
At sixty-five see halos and a swishing
Of light where clarity ought to be. The prize

For driving wrong tonight is one of those crosses
Along the roadway nobody stops to read.
The prize for loving wrong is one of those losses
We bring upon ourselves by being dead

Before we're dead. Tonight on Interstate Five
I squint and hope to get to Heaven alive.

LOVE IS A SHOTGUN

Love is a shotgun aimed at human hearts:
Blam! Blam! —you hear both barrels letting go,
And if the thing was loaded right, it starts
A dance that can't be ended till the snow

Has flown forever. The day you shot me dead,
Scattering my poor heart in all directions,
I picked the pieces up and went to bed,
Dreaming of nothing else but those confections

That form your body and your bon-bon soul.
Next morning I went walking in the Strand:
The wind was whistling through my gaping hole,
And passers-by, they stopped to shake my hand

And shake their heads. "Life is a loaded gun,"
I heard one say; "enjoy, enjoy! Have fun!"

THE WALNUT SHIP

I dripped some wax into a walnut shell
And stood my sturdy match-stick in the wax
To make a mast, and at the sound of the bell
I went to sea in a puddle by the tracks

Of the New York Central Railroad in the rain.
My ship sailed well for one that had no crew
And my brief sea was calm whenever the train
Was not around. But when it came I knew

The fiercest storms of all, and my poor craft,
It wallowed, pitched and rolled and all but sank.
I knew I stood too close, and yet I laughed
At all the dangers as my mind went blank.

The New York Central headed just my way.
And then? And then the heavens had their say.

MY UNCLE'S NAME OF SCHMIDT

Consider now my uncle's name of Schmidt:
Six consonants surround a trembling vowel,
Like prison guards above dark bricks that fit
Together, one on one, with mortar and trowel

To make a wall to keep the "I" inside,
As if afraid the lowly "I" might flee
And seek some other vowels with which to hide
In forests dark until such time as we

Have raised a rebel army to resist
This consonantal tyranny that means
To keep the lovely vowels from being kissed
By one another in this hill of beans

That we call life. Now cousin, let's go home.
Frankly, I'm sorry that I wrote this poem.

I'M JUST ALL THUMBS

When I'm around my Nan I'm just all thumbs,
Bumbling and clumsy as the sun is long,
Dropping my words like saltine cracker crumbs
Upon my shirt-front as I sing my song,

Or try to, anyway. She keeps me rattled,
My classical Nan does now, by being sweet
And rubbery as a rose. Well, I am addled
By love I guess whenever she takes a seat

Beside me on the couch to calmly watch
"Dateline" or "Sixty Minutes." You can call us
A couple of lovebirds now, unless I botch
This business once again. So please, Mike Wallace,

Don't ask too many questions this fine day.
Or better yet, shut up and go away.

HOW TO SAY MY NAME

Dear Nan, my name is Peter Thorpe. To say it,
You have to shut your mouth to make the "P,"
And then stick out your tongue so that you lay it
Gently against your teeth to get the "T"

And "H" effect, that sounds just like a lisp,
The kind that many a pre-school child might own.
Stick out your tongue and call the will o' the wisp,
The one whose name is Thorpe, who's made of bone

And flesh and sins. Remember, you can't say
My name unless you stick your tongue out, Nan,
Then clench your lips. There is no other way!
I hate my name and used to hate the man

Who gave it to me. When he headed south
He stuck his tongue out, then he shut his mouth.

VALENTINE TWO

A Valentine's a thing that should be sent
Only if all the feelings fall in line,
Only if what is said is what is meant,
And only if the sender has a sign

From deep inside his skull that he is guided
Not by his nether half but by his heart
And mind and soul. Dear Nan, I have decided
Mine own intentions are for real; mine art

Will now attempt to make some lines for you,
And maybe you'll forgive me if I fail,
Falling upon my face and turning blue.
So far this poem is prose, so weak and pale,

With only two lines left to make it right
—Well, make that *one*. Please come and spend the night!

MISS STRACH (IT RHYMES WITH SOCK)

Miss Strach was stricken by a stroke today
(Pretty she was, she was, when she was young);
It happened in the classroom, not the hay,
And now she can't move arm or hand or tongue.

Miss Strach was strict and sometimes angry too,
Throwing erasers at our drowsy heads
As down we drank the soporific goo
Of history books while thinking of the beds

We'd like to have the girls in. Pay attention!
Haven't you heard that poor Miss Strach has died?
She went through life, she went with no intention
Of giving away the thing she chose to hide.

And now we're wondering what it was we learned
From our Miss Strach, in crematorium burned.

BIODEGRADABLE LOVERS

We're biodegradable, Nan; even our clothes
Will slough away in a hundred years or so;
Yet when we reach the phase when no one knows
Just who we were and where we tried to go

In our brief lives, someone may come across
A couple of golden rings a couple of feet
Apart, beneath a soil all covered with moss
That managed to escape the searing heat

Of some black future century's nuclear strife.
This someone, if he's kind (or she) will know
There was a sharing here of limbs and life
By two who lived a thousand years ago

And loved a while and tried with all their might
To lift the ponderous curtains of the night.

DOODLING

I spent the evening doodling on a pad,
Mostly my memories of World War Two:
Black Messerschmitts and everything that's sad,
Barbed wire, Tojo's glasses, an aerial view

Of Solomon-Island jungles shot to hell,
And Hermann Goering partying in the slime.
This is an era you and I knew well,

Dear Nan, for we were living at that time,

Listening to FDR's luciferous chats,
A swatch of Tommy Dorsey, and some samples
Of Hitler on the air. We had six cats,
A dry apartment, and some fine examples

Of things that don't exist today, to wit:
Certainty, truth, and hope, and all that shit.

DEAD CENTER

Off of dead center I have moved but rarely
In these, my meat-loaf years, except to say
I more than once escaped from death, but barely,
By writing poems and rolling in the hay.

Dead center: that's the place to be when chance
No longer comes your way, when lovely legs
Bestow themselves on someone else's dance
And the strong man who bumps you suddenly begs

Your pardon, once the strong man sees you're old.
I'm resting on dead center like a frog
That hasn't moved all day, the color of gold
And hard to see in golden leaves and fog.

I'm staying put; dead center feels just right
For russet bones beneath the standstill night.

THE PUMPKIN TALKS

A jack o'lantern told me something once,
A couple of years ago, as I was walking
Along a darkened street: "You are a dunce,"
It said, "a dunce." I wondered who was talking,

For no one was around, or so I thought.
I saw the pumpkin lit by some low flame
Inside its sectioned head, ready to rot.
It sat upon a porch that had no name

And had some steps that time had rotted away.
I said, "Who said that now?" and "Who goes there?"
At first there was no answer, only the sway
And swish of trees against the midnight air.

And then there was the ancient voice once more:
"You are a dunce," it said. "You are a bore."

DOUBLE TAKE

The woman in the cocktail lounge was tall
And handsome too, with Barbara Stanwyck's features,
Forty or thereabouts, and slim and all
Aglow and talking with some guys —God's creatures

Seeking the thing they had to have, while she
Gave them the time of day but not much more,
Although they knew it not. She looked at me
A couple of times and smiled and almost tore

Myself away from me. But there was this:
Something about her movements and her hands,
Her too-strong hands, postponed the mental kiss
I was about to give her. Truth expands,

I guess, to fill the pattern and the plan:
This woman was no woman but a man.

ONE-DIMENSIONAL MAN

Approach me cynical, Nan, for what you see
Is only a standing life-size photograph
Mounted on cardboard, made to look like me,
Complete with speakers with my voice and laugh.

This is the one-dimensional fake I was
Before I found my Nan; this is the photo
That shows you what a shallow fellow does
Before he meets his dream. Dumb as a dodo,

This cardboard man should fall upon his face
And end up in the dumpster, if we fly
The way we should. And if we don't, the place
They have reserved for me after I die

Is deep and broad and filled with plenty of lime;
And I will go, and I'll have plenty of time.

LICK OF WORK

I didn't do a lick of work today.
I hardly stirred. I barely, barely moved
—Except to say I cut a load of hay
And made it into bales; and all I proved

Is that I failed to do a lick of work.
I laid some carpet in the family room
And patched the roof, and all I did was shirk
The duties I should do, so lower the boom

And punish me, dear Nan, give me a shove:
A man can hammer and dig and toil and toil,
But if he isn't working on his love
He's sitting on his duff. Boil me in oil,

Dear Nan, and shut our matrimonial doors;
Don't let me in until I've done my chores!

OLD CARPENTER'S LEVEL

I keep the bubble in the middle, Nan,
On this, my carpenter's level, that I place
Against these boards and bricks, according to plan,
As I attempt to build some things of grace.

First off, I'd like to build a house of trust
For us to live in for a thousand years,
And maybe a fence around it, for the lust
We mean to keep inside, and for the fears

We mean to keep away. See how this eye,
This greenish eye, of this old ebony level
That was my father's once, looks at the sky
When all is straight and true. There is no devil

That can come near us when we're resting straight
With drowsy hearts and nothing left to hate.

HAND ME THOSE CATALOGUES

Hand me those lavish catalogues, dear Nan,
And I shall send away for things for us;
We'll start with L.L. Bean: I have a plan
For ordering things for magic journeys, plus

Some things invisible that have no borders.
And let's consult Land's End; they have a flair
For handling dexterously the kinds of orders
We need to place for places high in the air

Where we might live when all our living's done.
I think it might be cold where we are going,
So let's get boots and hats. And if there's sun
That blazes down and never stops our knowing

That we have sinned, why then we will have seen
The last of old Land's End and L.L. Bean.

WHERE THE GIANT RAN

A hill of beans, dear Nan, a hill of beans:
It's hard to think we don't amount to that,
But Humphrey Bogart said so, and he means
Business, you know, and wears a slouching hat.

It broke his heart to put her on the plane
And watch her fly away; it breaks my heart
Simply to look at you, for I'm insane
About my Nan. I wish I had the art

To paint her right, to get the brush strokes right,
But all I have is beans, green and defiant,
Climbing against the sky to some great height
Where monsters live. And yet there is no giant

That's taller than our hill of love, dear Nan:
See these big footprints where the giant ran.

HEIL!

Here's a familiar face: it's somewhat square
When looked at one way, and it's sallow and round
When seen another way, and just what's there
In terms of soul and character can't be found

Above the ground. I say this man's a bumpkin
With angular mustache and a strut; he's spurious,
He's angry, hollow, paranoid, a pumpkin
With carved expressions. He can look so furious

That populations tremble at his name.
He'd just soon kill you off as look at you,
Unless you stoop, salute, and play his game
Over the face of Europe. I'm a Jew

Who chooses not to stand or wash his hair
Merely to please the hill of shit, this Herr.

MY POEM'S A BELL

Your curves, my darling Nan, are exponential,
Though that's a corny thing to say, I know;
It's just that you live up to your potential
And go beyond. You have so much to show,

And show it not, except to one who looks
Away, away, in order not to stare,
Except when told to: then four dozen books
Couldn't begin to tell what happens there,

When you and I are regular as a frame
That gets filled up and empties out again
And once again, and never holds the same
Within its bounds. My poem's a dark brown bell

That rings but once a century, if at all,
Unless, dear Nathalie, I hear your call.

I'M EMPTY LIKE A SHIP

I'm empty like a ship that's been unloaded:
My hull's half out of water; you can see
The brick-red paint, and I'm no longer bloated
With cargoes that mean not a thing to me.

When riding high at anchor with no plans
To put to sea or seek a destination,
You feel your life is free as any man's
And all is well. Then comes the hesitation,

The feeling that your freedom flies away
Because it isn't earned, and there's a canker
Upon the rose that blooms above the bay.
So hoist a heavy cargo, hoist your anchor,

And put to sea; forget about first light,
And go find Madagascar in the night.

AUNT AMELIA'S ASHES

My cousin sent me Aunt Amelia's ashes
All neatly packaged, like a hardback book;
There was a picture, with her long eyelashes
Seeming to bat themselves at all who'd look

Upon so vain a woman, under her wig,
So blonde and long, like Jayne's or Norma Jean's.
Amelia saw herself as something big,
And here she is the size of coffee beans

From Starbuck's, half a pound, and dark as mud.
Why did you leap, dear Aunt Amelia, why?
And did you hit the sidewalk with a thud?
They say that as you fell you gave a cry,

Something about a mess of scrambled eggs,
A bowl of mush, some toast, some twisted legs.

HOW DID YOU

How did you get to where you got to, Nan?
I mean, how did you get your shapely mind
And your intelligent legs and breasts? Whose plan
Was following you, and was it close behind?

And how, if you don't mind my asking, dear,
Did you acquire your smile, your Irish smile?
I'll bet the Blarney Stone is hurrying near
To fetch another kiss and stay a while

Upon your calm commensurate lips, while I
Stop, look, and listen, here at Heaven's Gate,
Where willingly I would wait until the sky
Falls hard upon our April heads. Oh wait!

I quite forgot to mention something —no,
On second thought, forget it, let it go.

SENIOR MOMENTS

What did we do last Tuesday, darling Nan?
Did we go shopping? Did we stay at home?
And did we strike a boy or trip a man?
I wonder if we spent the day in Rome?

Maybe we saw the slaves but failed to free 'em,
Maybe we robbed a bank and shot some guards,
Maybe we tried to blow the Colosseum
To Kingdom Come, in both of our back yards.

Whatever the case may be, I'll bet we had
A high old time. I wish I could remember
What year it was and where we were. I'm glad
You have a better grip on things. December

Goes on for sixty days, with everything iced,
And too much laughter, for the love of Christ.

ON LOVE-MAKING

A yoke that's not a yoke: that's what your feet
Create whenever they're resting on my shoulders;
And like a slow ox plowing soil for wheat,
I slog for love and steer around the boulders

The best I can, while your soft busy hands
Traffic my hair. These boulders: are they there
As strict reminders that we came from lands
Where nothing was ever spiritual and fair?

And your soft hands: what signals do they send,
Here in the night where thoughts have arms and legs?
Steering around these boulders makes us bend
A thousand ways: it's all that passion begs.

Come morning, I will find you at the sink
In our dark kitchen. Plenty of time to think.

IN A CHRISTMAS STOCKING

These damp and foggy mornings are for talking
With Nan about the kinds of things that toys
Might chat about inside the Christmas stocking
While waiting for the yelps of girls and boys.

Christmas is too commercial, say the preachers
On Sunday mornings, while we lie in bed,
Our limbs criss-crossed. We are the practical teachers
And students of each other; we are dead

Unless we love, and whether Christmas flies
But once a year or every other day,
It's Yuletide every morning in our eyes
Because of you-know-what. And so we say:

Leave us alone inside this sock of love;
Here's where the jolly hawk becomes a dove.

THE WEASEL-WORM

I'm not an artist; I'm an actual man
Who imitates the artist at his easel;
I'm not a lion in the jungle, Nan;
I simply wear his mane, for I'm a weasel

Strutting upon the sidewalks of deceit,
Dressed in a tux and tie and looking natty
And trying to dance according to the beat
That's in the woods just south of Cincinnati,

Where all this action is and was to be.
I sneak along the sidewalks inch by inch,
Hoping to Christ that no one steps on me
And makes me feel the pain, the punitive pinch.

Sorry to be so tardy with this thing;
When you have read these lines, give me a ring.

FOR WALT AND SUSIE

We damn near broke our necks this morning, Walt,
Climbing out of the bathtub hand in hand;
We slipped; it wasn't anybody's fault,
And Nan knew how to fall and how to land,

So we weren't hurt at all. Nan says that marriage
Is knowing how to land and knowing when
To trade the Porsche in for a horse and carriage
While standing tall and growing young again.

Marriage, it seems to us, is heaven on earth,
A feathery nest of love that can't be beat,
A mellowing mix of meanings and of mirth,
And never a freeway but a two-way street.

This you and Susie know as girl and boy:
Congratulations now! Enjoy, enjoy!

AFTER SKIING WITH WHOSE WIFE

We stopped to get a bite to eat in Vail,
After a day of skiing in the Highlands
And kissing on the chairlift. You looked pale
Although you had a sunburn. There was silence,

No mention of the adulterous thing that took
Much longer than it lasted. The waiter, tan,
A ski-bum with a sullen walk, a look
So cold that one might draw it with a crayon,

Seemed put-upon, as though we wasted his time
Instead of our own. He served us stew. We ate.
You left no tip. We drove. We had to climb

The Continental Divide, and we were late.

I dropped you at the park-and-ride with ease.
You walked away, lugging your slender skis.

UNORIGINAL MAN

I'm the original unoriginal man,
Standing upon my head to get attention
On Flatbush Avenue, by a garbage can,
With people hurrying by who'll never mention,

When they get home, the piteous thing they've seen:
A man of sixty with a face as red
As fatuous stoplights, and a mind as green
As any child's. And when they get to bed,

These folks who've seen my unoriginal act
Will give me not a single thought, unless
They too have mixed a fiction with a fact
And stood upon their heads. You wore a dress

When you first saw me, did you not? And why
Did you pass up the chance to pass me by?

TWO HEADS ARE BETTER

Two heads are better, Nathalie, than one,
Just as a single heart is better than two
When two are joined for life and day is done
And you are me, dear Nan, and I am you.

Let us stroll hand in hand, or better yet,
Let us combine our bodies for a walk
Up on top of the mountain where it's wet,
With melting snows and pine trees that can talk.

What will the pine trees tell us of our hearts?
And will they tell us how the future looks
And just exactly when our life departs?
Oh, we don't want to know! We'll read no books

That tell of times to come. Let's close our eyes!
Who needs to read these melancholy lies?

BOTHERING MY WIFE

Be sure to drink your juice this morning, Nan;
    We're going to need some energy today,
    To deal with all the problems facing man
    (And women too) since time got underway.

But first things first: I'm going to hold you down
    And tickle you until you laugh and scream
    Like someone stuffed away in Looney Town,
    Where all the best of Bedlam only seem

To be as mad as you and I. Who knows,
But God, who needs to be locked up in there
And who should freedom have? An ill wind blows
    The loonies to and fro, tickling the air

With problems of mankind. We're half insane
When tickling thus, as if we shared a brain.

WITH MY OWN WORDS

Last night I fell in love with my own words:
They knocked upon my bedroom door at three
And then flew at me like a thousand birds
In the old Hitchcock movie. I could see

They'd kill me if I didn't love them right
And put them into poems that none could read
Except the singers who keep love in sight,
Looking through windows where the raindrops bead.

Last night I fell on top of my own vowels
And consonants while trying to write for you
A piece made out of bricks with shiny trowels
Dipped in the waters of my heart so blue.

I fell in love with language, Nan, last night;
I fished till dawn and never got a bite.

WINTER LOVERS

Summer's a goner, Nan, and so am I;
I love you past the point of no return;
Believe me, love, I'd scarcely bat an eye
If all the planets suddenly started to burn,

So long as I could keep on holding you
And kissing your white legs the way we kissed
The first time that we loved and woke at two,
Ready to go again. I made a fist

And you compressed it hard between your thighs;
It was so hot there that I thought my hand
Would melt, and I felt tears riding my eyes.
You spoke of passion and about the land

And how it had no lovers anymore,
Except the two of us upon the floor.

SPIDERS WITH WINGS

Spiders with wings, I've got some spiders with wings
That scurry and buzz inside my skull and drive
My mind outside my mind, which usually brings
An itch that can't be scratched, a big beehive

That can't be emptied out, a brown ant hill
Inside my soul that can't be kicked apart,
Or maybe a grayish papery nest to fill
With angry wasps who come and sting my heart

And never seem to cease. There's no way out
Except the usual way, and that's to be
So much in love with Nan that there's no clout
In all my fears and foibles. Nan, you see,

Has made me and unmade me to remake me
In such a way that no one else can take me.

I QUIT SMOKING

I smoked for decades, Nan, three packs a day,
Luckies and Camels mostly, and some Kools
Whenever I felt my throat was going away,
Back in those cold-war days when work was play,

Or so it seems in retrospect. My God,
The way I tried to rob myself of breath
Day after day, I should be under the sod,
Yet here I stand and wiggle my nose at death.

I liked the way that Humphrey Bogart smoked,
Cupping the Chesterfield within his hand
And wincing (never smiling) as he poked
The butt into the ashtray —while the band

At Ciro's played some sentimental song
To help the carcinomas move along.

THE SENIOR COUPLE SITS OUTSIDE

This is a perfect day to sit outside
And watch the boats go by on Puget Sound;
This island no one's heard of, and the tide
Moves slow and flat, as if there were no ground

Under the tide. The slate-gray wavelets crawl
Like wrinkles in our senior-citizen skins
In gentle winds. A sloop, a ketch, a yawl,
And maybe some dolphins now and then, whose fins

Resemble gentle hatchets —these we see
Whenever we wake from dozing in our chairs
After a bourbon lunch. You look at me
And I at you, and we know no one cares

About our love except the two of us.
(Sometimes we talk and sometimes we discuss.)

I WORE A SIDE-ARM ONCE

I wore a side-arm once, just for a day,
A big chrome wooden-handled Colt revolver
Which heavily rode my hip like lumps of clay
Dragging upon the ground. A problem-solver

I thought I was, until my accurate wife
Took me aside and gave me a little talk:
"Problems are never solved when someone's life
Is threatened, dear heart, or whenever we walk

With swaggering steps and faces crammed with force;
Problems are often solved by solving not,
If damage done is greater than the source"
—And then she smiled and fetched the coffee pot.

I thought on this the rest of Christmas day,
And then I put my frivolous gun away.

MARITAL LAUGHTER

Serious bone in your body, you don't own
A serious bone, my daft and darling Nan,
Except when we are huddling all alone
There in the back of vast eternity's van,

Hatching our plans for spring and summer and fall
—How to survive while parceling out our breath
Between those glorious laughing jags that all
Good marriages are fashioned with till death.

The day that we stop laughing, that's the day
The Leaning Tower of Babel tries to hide
Inside our mouths, for there's no other way
For serious love to live. When Plato tried

To snuff that tender snickering with his laws,
The world fell over with its loud guffaws.

JOHN WAYNE AND GAIL RUSSELL

"Wake of the Red Witch," it was called, an old
John Wayne-Gail Russell sultry kind of thing
Of fifty years ago: a ship with hold
Bulging with treasure sinks, and he must bring

The bullion to the surface, not without
Grappling a giant octopus, and yes,
Dark kisses from a girl who baked a pout
Into a smile and wore a filmy dress.

I was fourteen and wild and went to see
The movie seven times, led by an id
And super-ego that encompass me
Down to this very day. A giant squid

All wrapped around you in the night is fine,
When you are old and memories break your spine.

JUST CALL THEM PUMPKIN EATERS

Here come the pumpkin eaters down the street,
Licking their lips and lolling with their eyes;
Where will they land tonight? Where will they eat?
—In some dark bistro where the menu lies?

Ah, send them down the valley of the pines,
Where no wind ever blows, except the breeze
That stirs along my skin and then declines
To just a whisper as you move your knees

And clasp my naked back with open palms.
The pumpkin eaters never learned a thing
In all their days, except the thing that calms
Our restive blood. Now you can hear them sing:

We are the pumpkin men, the ravenous men;
We've done this since we can't remember when.

LESS THAN FIFTY PER CENT

PEANUTS

I bought a can of mixed and salted nuts
And spread them out upon a yellowish platter;
My mind, it said no if's and and's and but's,
As I began to count. Now here's the matter:

The label says there's less than fifty per cent
Of peanuts in the can, and I had doubts;
But when I counted these legumes, hell bent
On getting angry at the packager's touts,

I found the peanuts there far less than half
And plenty of almonds, cashews, and a high
Brazil nut shaped like someone's foot. The laugh
Was on me then. I laughed, then started to cry.

That's when I picked the telephone up and dialed
Your number, just to hear the way you smiled.

WE SHARED A CANDY BAR

We shared a candy bar, a Milky Way,
I think it was —it was so long ago.
It might have been a Mars or something they
No longer make. And we stood toe to toe,

Each one with half a candy bar in the mouth
And lips engaged in a chocolate-flavored kiss,
While our four hands drove east and west and south
To find some naked places for our bliss.

We had a candy bar, Three Musketeers,
I think it was, in fragmentary weather;
There were three sections to it, and our years,
The sense that comes with time, kept them together

—Down to this very night, when it's so cold
That no one knows that no one knows we're old.

THE MOVIE STAR IN THE PANTRY

Elizabeth Taylor spoke to me in a dream,
Standing by tins of tuna in the pantry;
I stood by cans of evaporated cream
And told her she was great in "Elmer Gantry."

She frowned and said she didn't make that one,
And so I said I liked her "Elephant Walk,"
To which she said she hated that hot sun
And all the sticky-stink and foreign talk.

I cut our conversation short: my Nan
Was calling me, and dreams just lead you on
To somewhere's nowhere, where a half a can
(You follow me? I thought I saw a yawn)

Of tuna is a full one, though it's not,
And one can't think of things he thought he thought.

THE WOMAN LIAR

I used to know a pathological liar;
In fact, I married her on a day of rain;
For what she had to sell there was no buyer
Except myself. By Christ, she had a brain

Three-fifths invention and the rest all guile,
To take you in and let you out again
In a day-long rain. She had a radiant smile
With dangerous radiation that was sin;

She had some expertise in being true
But opted not to use it; she had some
Abilities in the field of being blue
Whenever she made it with a useless bum

And tried to cover it up. I don't know how
I missed her, but I did until just now.

ON THE DEATH OF JFK, JR.

The thing that he was soon to be has fled,
Like some white rabbit into a nether place;
And now some part of some of us is dead
For a week or maybe a month. We see the face,

The affable face, the hair, the boyish stammer,
The eyes set wide as headlights on a Rolls,
Bright as a sailboat's sail, as if the hammer
Of fate was not about to fall: it tolls

And tolls and tolls —the bell, I mean, the gong
That tells us of his going. Let him pass,
Good people, stand aside; he's done no wrong,
And now he's stepping through the looking glass

Into a land where all the scenery parts
To make a path for Kings and Queens of Hearts.

REMEMBERING JFK, JR.

Go through all this again? We simply can't
(And yet we must) go through. The horse-dark hair,
The burnished eyes set wide, the grins that grant
Cool interviews now and then, slouched in a chair,

As though he wasn't someone and the only
Male remnant of the royalty in the States:
What kind of future sank there in that lonely
Black stretch of sea? The country speculates:

A smiling liberal senator? A place
On cabinets? An ambassador's credential?
A handsome failure? A presidential face?
How do we measure one when one's potential

Outlives the man? And should there be a flame
To mark the man whose century never came?

ON YOUR KNEE

You're a ventriloquist and I'm a dummy
Whenever I'm on your knee and you have hands
Beneath my jacket, one hand on my tummy,
The other behind my back, on leather bands

That work my jaw and eyelids. You know what
I'm going to say before I have a clue:
With stiff mechanical lips and face that's cut
From hemlock trees and painted with a hue

One finds upon a doctored corpse, I start:
The words fall out from somewhere, and I hear
Myself deliver promises from the heart
Although it's not my heart. You move me, dear,

In all the wrong directions. And this clown,
He loves you much too much to hop on down.

FECKLESS IN SEATTLE

I stand tonight on University Bridge,
Looking through rain at university lights
From forty years ago. And many a ridge
I've climbed since then, but always with my sights

Set far too low, and always with my hands
Grasping at straws or grasping at the wind.
I had success at home, in foreign lands,
And in the minds of others. Yet I sinned

In sinning not: I mean, I made the bark
That every other dog was making, standing
On hinder legs and cursing at the dark,
And making nothing new and understanding

Nothing. And on the bridge there's nothing to fear:
I wonder what the fuck I'm doing here.

DIVORCE PAPERS

My new and cost-an-arm-and-a-leg TV:
It has a "picture in a picture" feature
So you can watch an old romance and see
A boxing match, a liar, or some creature

Caught in a net and thrashing for its life
All at the same and very time. I think
It's emblematic of our age that strife
And gentleness can use a similar ink

And play so well upon this competent screen,
Here in this semi-darkened house where gloom
And silence, Shirley Anne, are all I've seen
—Since yesterday, when you were in this room

Just long enough to place your final stricture,
Making me just a picture in a picture.

THOUGHTS ON A DISASTER AT SEA

Some days I'm down and some dark days I'm manic,
Up like a kite and crammed with off-beat truths;
On some mean days I think about the Titanic
And what went wrong and how so many youths

And pretty ones went down. I wasn't ice
That brought her deep, nor faulty navigation,
Nor Captain Smith's Alzheimer's, nor the dice
The gods all threw to make a situation

That jettisoned fifteen hundred souls that day.
Some say the steel was brittle; some say no,
It was the speed and bulk of the thing; some say
The Bible knows. Or was it just the show,

The pomp, the strut, the smirking arrogant pride
Of smokestack egos resting under the tide?

LEGLESS VETERAN

Mentally on my tiptoes all day long,
Afraid to speak or laugh or sing or smile,
With fingers crossed, I hope to hear the song
Your voice can make in just a little while

If you decide to come tonight. The way
Lies through the woods; be sure to tread with care;
There may be snakes and pitfalls —as they say,
The road to love is there, and then not there.

I hope you make it. I will roll my chair
As far as it can travel on this porch
And peer into the woods with half a pair
Of warrior's eyes. My heart will be a torch

You may not see. Take care. Don't lose your knees
The way I did when I was overseas.

MONDAY IN BETHLEHEM PARK

I spent the morning playing with my kids,
Out by the swings and slide and teeter-totter
Above the steel mill. Cumulus clouds were lids
About to close and rain, and son and daughter

Kept glancing at the sky as they went riding
Furiously on the swings, as though pursued
By some dark circus bear who had been hiding
Under their beds. Perhaps it was my mood,

Perhaps it was the years I spent in the mill:
I sat down on the lower end of the slide
And put my head in my hands —while down the hill,
The mill sat rusting. And as my son cried,

My daughter swung up high and gave a whoop,
Trying to reach the sky and loop the loop.

IN THE CATSKILLS

Stand-up comedians have a job to do:
Each night they sketch a topsy-turvy world;
Some get applauded and some get a boo,
Some find success, and just as many are hurled

Like over-ripe tomatoes against a wall,
A wall of silence. Here's a fellow from Yonkers:
He does John Wayne impressions with a drawl
And teetering walk. The audience goes bonkers

And laughs itself to death. The next comedian
Is clever as all get-out, but the crowd
Won't laugh. They yawn. They think he's much too meaty and
A bore to boot. He's dirty and too loud.

They start to throw things. He flips them the bird.
He wonders what went wrong. He hasn't heard.

AT REST

The sky is silk, with neither bird nor cloud,
    As I repose today. It can't be named,
This feeling that I have; it rings so loud
In my cold brain and makes me feel ashamed

    Of what I can't recall. It's hard to think
About a thing that can't be thought of. Brains
    Are not supposed to fail, run out of ink,
    And yet they do. The little electric trains

That raced from cell to cell within my thoughts
Have stopped, and all the engineers have gone
    Into the earth to seek forget-me-nots.
    And I will not remember this till dawn

    When I awake and suddenly recall
    That I can't move, or anything at all.

THE OLD LOVER'S LAMENT

I'm Peter Peter pumpkin eater now,
Left in the wake of many a young man's ship
That leaves me standing like a garbage scow
That's carrying things that no one wants: a lip

That hasn't kissed for oh I don't know how
And many lonesome moons, a fingertip
That hasn't touched a woman's breast or brow
For far too long, an old arthritic hip

That can no longer dance or scrape or bow,
A couple of rheumy eyes that always slip
From focus now except when watching the Dow,
And hands that tremble like a buggy whip.

So put another shot across my bow:
No Peter pumpkin eater am I now.

LOVELY FORTYISH
HOUSEWIFE

Beyond my wildest dreams it wasn't so wild
As I'd expected: tried for eighteen weeks
To get her into bed: one day she smiled
And told me yes and kissed me on both cheeks,

Starting us off. But somehow there was less
Of passion's Fourth-of-July than any man
Might look for in the illicit word of "yes"
Beneath the bedclothes by her husband's tan

And handsome portrait on the nightstand there,
Beside the alarm. What should have been a thrill,
If only for the danger, was but fair
To middling now, beneath the grassy hill.

Ecstasy should have been there; but, you know,
I think I'm glad that it refused to show.

I'D NEVER SEEN HER BEFORE

Prerogatives? I have none, unless one counts
My memories of the way we met and fell
Headlong in love. You've seen a panther pounce?
Nothing at all, compared to our pell-mell

Kissing and clutching on that subway train
Under the river on our way to Queens
So late at night as strangers going insane
And no one else around. I said, "This means

We'll spend our years together till the end,
Talking and laughing, sending for the stork
Again and again." But you said, "No, my friend,
Your lips were sweet, but isn't this New York?

I mean to sadden a thousand men before
I bow and turn my back and shut the door."

THE DEPRESSED FIGHTER PILOT

The fighter pilots saunter to their planes,
Carrying white helmets under their arms. It's hot
In the Nevada sun. "It fries your brains,"
The skipper says. The others hear him not

Because he bores them. He is short, unskilled
In social things, though skilled enough in flight.
He's had some knocks: his wife is getting killed
By cancer, and at thirty-nine his sight

Is failing, and they'll ground him pretty soon
And give him some damn desk job in D.C.
He likes Nevada in the middle of June:
Mirages turn the runway into a sea

And make things walk on water. And his wife
Will slip. And he'll need reasons for his life.

BREASTS IN FIRELIGHT

What's missing in this picture? Here's a man
And here's a woman dancing under a tree,
And here's a piece of rope that thinks it can
Become a snake, and here's an open sea

With nary a ship in sight, and here's a sky
The color of a battleship. What's missing
Are sights and sounds and smells and things that I
Must write about when we are finished kissing.

I love your lips, dear lady; they're so pink;
I crave the way they softly part for me
And let me taste your soul. I cannot think
Without some thoughts of you. I want to see

Your naked breasts in firelight when you're ready,
And in the meantime I'll be holding steady.

UNRULY SONNETS

Hi! My name's Peter Thorpe, and I write sonnets
    —Or try to, anyway. It doesn't take long:
It's just a matter of finding the right bonnets
    To put upon these baby words. A song

Should start in infancy and then should grow
    Briskly like plantain weeds in a king's lawn,
Until there's no grass left. A sonnet should show
    How something we don't know is going on,

Is going on within ourselves. Pete Thorpe's
    Unruly sonnets always attempt this feat
And sadly often fail. Like many a corpse,
    They will lie flat with tags upon their feet,

Until enlivened by some lover's breath
—For how else shall these words be kept from death?

FOR A FRIEND WITH PARKINSON'S DISEASE

Motor control: that's what it's all about,
This shit disease that shakes our friends away
Before they're even gone and makes us doubt
That God can talk or that he knows the Way.

I saw a photo of Cape Cod this morning,
Taken from sixty quivering miles in space;
It looked so small: could God without a warning
Destroy it and leave nothing in its place?

No, I don't think so. That would take some thought,
And God is simply wavering at this time;
He merely lets us quake and sink and rot
While indices of hate and anger climb.

Cape Cod: it lunges east and north and south.
It takes the words right out of heaven's mouth.

THE KITTENS AND OUR MOTHER

Our kittens climbed behind the dresser drawers
And settled among the socks and underwear
For a winter's nap. We looked on all three floors
Of our cold house and could not find a hair.

It was as if they'd gone to another land,
But mother said, "Don't worry, they'll appear
Soon as I start the pot roast, soon as my hand
Shuts the refrigerator, they'll be here,

Pretending to be starved. You'll hear the mews
Everywhere then." Oh, but our mother was wrong!
Our furry friends had died —that was the news
Our mother gave us later, singing a song

To cheer us some. She went behind a cloud,
Or so it seemed to us, and sang too loud.

JFK, JR., AGAIN

We watched the coverage on TV: the plane
Had vanished in the night, and we were down.
  He was a jovial sort and much the main
Escutcheon still alive in Kennedy Town,

  The modern House of Atreus with a roof
Comprised of tears and sobs and many an issue
  Yet to be born. The funeral horse's hoof
Must stumble once again, and blood and tissue

And bits of bone and brain-stuff will be gone,
Packaged and wrapped by media folk and made
  Somehow presentable, and we'll go on.
We will be sad. The comer's dead. The blade

  Is not so gay, that might have perched atop
A capitol or a flagpole. All must stop.

ASSASSINATIONS

Where were you, Nan, when JFK was lost?
And Bobby too, and Martin Luther King?
And Lady Di, who tried to melt the frost?
And where were you when you first felt the sting

Of our new love? It seems we always know
Just where we were when shocking things transpired
Or where we are when true love starts to show
And there's a glowing there. What I admired

Back then, before I knew you, lost its shine
In half the time it takes to blink my hand,
Soon as I dared to hope you might be mine
And felt the surge that suddenly floods the land

Of love. No need to build an ark, dear Nan;
We'll simply swim until we reach Japan.

I'M FAMOUS

I'm famous, so to speak; I'm known in barns
Where nickering horses seek my sugary touch;
I'm known in parks, where seniors spin their yarns
And ask me for a couple of bucks (not much).

Folks recognize my face (sometimes) on streets
Where beggars congregate to read our palms,
And also in bright places where one meets
The high society sneers that fall like bombs.

There's scarcely any place where I'm not known,
Long as we're talking places no one knows,
Places where crowds confirm that you're alone
And walking against a wind that never blows.

I'm famous in a way that fame can't know;
I'll have some sugar for you when you go.

DOWN MOOD

I had a chance to sing and turned it down;
To dance, and simply sat upon my thumbs;
They offered me free nights upon the town
And all I did was hang around with bums.

I heard the opportunities knocking hard
Upon my plywood door: I didn't budge;
A game of solitaire with one last card
To play, a cigarette, a plate of fudge

Preoccupied me as I sat and let
The stinking world roll by; I didn't care
If hell froze over. Want to make a bet
I changed my tune? I didn't, and I dare

That stinking world to prove that I was wrong
Or that the life I lead will last that long.

LET ME GO HUNTING NOW

Let me go hunting now, and let me find,
Never the bear, the boar, or African cat,
But rather those things that make me frail of mind:
Vanities, starchy thoughts, and all the fat

That grows beneath my scalp when I'm not home.
Let me go hunting now, and let me seek
Some semblance of my genuine self: a poem
That comes right from the gut and not the meek

Unvisceral universe of popular air.
Let me go stand beside the purling stream
And lean upon my listless rifle there
Until I wake, dear Nan, from this dull dream.

Then five will get you ten that twenty kisses
Will ride upon the eyelash of my Mrs.

HANDSOME IS

Mother said, "Handsome is as handsome does,"
And Dad was handsome in his boots but sailed
For Shanghai early on: he knew what was
And what was not his role. My father mailed

A couple of picture postcards from some place
I'd never heard of, while my Mom attempted
To put on all a satisfactory face,
While rain came down and youth and growth pre-empted

Much further thought of family and all that.
I went out into worlds of men, like Stanley
In search of Livingston; I wore a hat
You might see on safaris; I was manly,

Or so I thought, but wasn't a handsome man
Until I met and married my sweet Nan.

JOAN CRAWFORD, SYDNEY GREENSTREET

Joan Crawford just shot Sidney Greenstreet, Nan,
And there he lies, in a pool of blood that's black
In this old black-and-white, comes-in-a-can,
Dull formulaic film, with smoker's hack

Emerging from the eloquent jowls of Sydney.
We watch this film together, Nan, ensconced
Here on our crimson love-seat. He died, didn't he?
—And yet he lives, on screen. The thing he wants,

Pointing a pudgy finger at our faces,
Is just for us to stay in love and live
Together always, riding in such places
Where avenues are green. May these days give

To us the best of woman and of man,
Slow-turning, like a Casablanca fan.

GREEN HORNET, ETC.

"Who knows what evil lurks" —I liked the way
Those elder radio programs caught my mind
On rainy nights when I had hit the hay
And lay tucked in and safe, hoping to find

The strength to catch the monsters in my head.
Batman, Green Hornet, Superman, and all
Those old bold beaters of the horse that's dead:
I must salute you now, although I call

Your cellophane names from fifty years away.
I must salute you now; I must confess
I let you down; I threw my guts away
And towed the line and sank my manliness.

I should have been somebody, don't you think?
Let me talk on, my love, there's plenty of ink.

THE PATIENT

I stood awhile and looked into my grave,
All freshly dug, so dark, so damp, so deep,
So happily shaped, rectangular and brave
(In view of what was coming there to sleep),

With small white roots cut off and sticking out
Like rodents' legs from the four silent walls:
I waxed ebullient with a silent shout
And leaped into my grave to see if Paul's

"Through a glass darkly" had some application
To what I was about to do. The sky
Was empty, and I had no obligation
To tell it anything. I cast my eye

Upon the floor and smelled the black-brown earth
And listened to the pancreatic mirth.

ON SMILING AND LAUGHING

Gassed up my Ford and drove a couple of miles
To K-Mart, where I bought a couple of shirts;
Looked at some Timex watches too, with smiles
From clerks who know that smiling often hurts

When it's the only option of the day.
I've never seen you smile, my better half,
Unless some better thought has found its way
Between your mind and mouth. And you will laugh

Only at what is laughable, not foul.
You study to avoid those stark arenas
Where crowds of empty-heads are made to howl
And laugh at anything, like dull hyenas

Who hang around the kill at crack of dawn,
Waiting for all the lions to be gone.

FYI

Just for your information, Nan, I've moved
(Within my mind, I mean), and now I dwell
On Madeleine Street, where no one's ever proved
That love can't last or that there's even a hell.

And though I've moved to this posh neighborhood
(Within my flesh, I mean), we're just as near,
Physically, as we were when we first stood
Tiptoe to toe and kissed without the fear

.

That lovers sometimes feel when starting out.
We knew our pink procedures and we knew
That all we needed to learn was how to doubt
The ones who say that love can't last. Oh you!

You made me move to Madeleine Street today,
Dear Nan, and you and I are here to stay

THE FLAVOR HILL

I spent the morning flat upon my face
Right in the midst of traffic on I-5,
Just south of San Clemente, over a place
They call the Flavor Hill. I stayed alive

By kicking and by flailing both my arms,
Making the kindly, angry drivers swerve
And swear; I kept my body out of harm's
Loud way by concentrating on the nerve

That hooks me to the Flavor Hill and makes me
Fall through the pavement's cracks and keep on falling
Until I touch the top. Then fancy takes me
Much farther down, to where Mack trucks are hauling

Huge scoops of sherbet (lemon and lime) to fill
The valleys and the caves of Flavor Hill.

THE COLLAR

The day my father passed away I laughed
And couldn't stop. I laughed so hard I cried;
   I fell back on the bed, and fore and aft
I rocked myself, and then from side to side.

   It was as if the walls had walked away,
   Leaving the winds to walk across my soul,
   To make me new and fresh again. My day
Was made that day, and suddenly I was whole

   —Or so I thought. For even as I roared,
   There was a something standing by the bed,
   As dim and huge and militant as a chord
Struck on an old pipe organ when the dead

   Are put away. The thing said nothing at all.
   It simply stood. I went and made my call.

TO ELEANOR, WHO DUMPED ME

Staying on even keel's a full-time job,
Since January first, the day you left
With Fred or George or Joe or was it Bob
—I can't remember which. My mind's bereft

Of memories, thoughts and feeling. All I know
Is that you're gone the way a ship is gone
After it stands on end and slips below,
With strong sailors going under the dawn.

Staying on even keel: I don't know how
I'll manage but I will. Maybe I'll find
Some plain-brown-wrapper woman who will wow
Me every night in bed and not remind

My riveted brain of you. She'll make me feel
The way I should when I'm on even keel.

THE ENGINEER

I was an engineer in a previous life,
Designing things to make small things go well
Between a man and mate; there was no strife
—Before this engineer went all to hell.

I asked the Lord for help; I prayed with verve,
Stopping beside the road in my blue Ford
With my head bowed in a way I thought would serve
To send God back again to the drawing board

To find me something new —a face perhaps,
Maybe some manners or a brand-new wallet,
Or possibly the friendship of some chaps
Who'd tell me how to win your whatchamacallit.

Jehovah never answered me; my flattery
Went nowhere. All I got was a dead battery.

DYIN'

I've got some bullets in me and I'm dyin'
Here on the prairie floor just west of Dodge;
The boys who robbed the bank, they caught me lyin'
And told their dirty bullets where to lodge.

My Nan, she knows I should be home by now
And wonders where I lie or where I stand;
She wonders why I haven't milked the cow
Or chopped the wood or plowed our patch of land.

Come spring, I think I'll still be lyin' here,
My bones picked clean by animals and sun;
My Nan, she'll cry, she'll dry, she'll wait a year,
And maybe she'll marry again. And maybe my gun

Will rust. God bless! I hope she'll think of me
Whenever the wind blows through the jack pine tree.

A SENIOR IN LONG'S DRUGSTORE

A drugstore is a way of life for those
Who have no life, a way of life for some
Who've been around too long and have a nose
And ears grown big with age and legs too clum-

Sy. Show the young Hispanic clerk that you
Can still walk straight without your cane and can't,
And she will laugh behind your face. A Jew
Of seventy-five, a Jewish man, must grant

That all the world at this late stage has shrunk
Into a ball, a turnip you can stuff
Into your pocket, walking like a drunk
And thinking, idiot, you have done enough.

He stops to look at calculators now:
Only five bucks. The morning takes a bow.

THE DAVENPORT MAN

Keeping my nose clean is a tough assignment,
Especially with my background, darling Nan;
But I will toe the marriage-vow's alignment
Because I'd like to be a davenport man.

A davenport man's a man who never moves
From where he is supposed to be, unless
His wife has smiled and told him to, which proves
He doesn't have to, nor does she, I guess,

Long as the love is there among the pillows
Upon the davenport where I will stay
Until there's no more wind among the willows,
Until there's no more night and no more day.

A davenport man's a man whose love is steady
On all occasions, Nan. I'm here. I'm ready.

NO HELP FROM PLATO

A copy of a copy of a copy:
That's what these lines are, frail and far removed
From Plato's town. I've filled a five-inch floppy
With metrical chaff, my love, and all I've proved

Is how commensurate is a thing I heard:
You're not supposed to write about your writing.
Oh hell, I'll go ahead, my vision blurred,
I guess, by being bit instead of biting,

My passions in a Windsor knot, my reason
Hobnobbing with my instincts, and my fashions
Looking a dry millennium out of season.
Sir Conscience says I must have left my passions

Under a spiral notebook in the poppies,
Where birds and bees make copies out of copies.

TRASH COMPACTOR

My memory is a trash compactor, Nan
—Eggshells and coffee grounds and cartons too,
And now and then a letter from a man
Who knew a woman once I thought I knew

Before the "you and I" became the "us."
I've tamped these memories down a thousand times,
So that there'd be no baggage and no fuss
—Yet sometimes in my sleep I hear the chimes

The ass-hound hears at midnight when he's late
And lying through his teeth. All this I place
Down in the trash compactor of my hate.
To smithereens and hell I send his face,

This womanizing ape I used to be
Before you talked and taught me to be free.

ABOUT A FOOTBALL WIDOW

The Chargers are ahead this afternoon;
So are the Saints, the Jets, and Buffalo Bills;
I pour my medicine into a spoon,
The stuff that saves your life and almost kills.

And settling back to watch the Raiders scoff
At clumsy handlings by some slow, slow team
Whose name evades my brain as I drift off,
I start to dream of Nan. I start to dream

Of the Boston girl who wears redoubtable smiles
When things are tough or raw or stale or mean,
Even when all my moods are black, with miles
To go before the kick-off. I have seen

My Nan perform such miracles as make
My burnished heart remember what's at stake.

I'M BOOKISH LATELY

I'm bookish lately: studying is my forte;
Tolstoy and Dostoyevsky, yes, but faces
I'm reading too, as if to learn to sort
The honest from the "not" public places

Like pubs and crowded buses and the schools
Where ordinary-looking boys with packs
Are carrying who-knows-what and breaking rules
Before the rules are made. If you can fax

To me before the morning comes, dear Nan,
The answers to the questions of the looks
That can't be read by those who usually can,
I'll send my love to you in portable books

That only you can read in crowds of strangers,
Even while babes are smothering in their mangers.

JOAN BLONDELL AND RELATED MATTERS

Of Joan Blondell we've seen the last, I guess,
Joan Crawford too, and Lana T., and Liz,
And all the other stars who used to dress
As if preparing to undress. Show biz,

It has its quaint come-hithery hype; but, Nan,
There's more to life than laughs that are not meant
Or tears that come from onions, not from man
Or woman. Hey, when we're on passion bent

We need no guidance from those studio elves
Who ride upon a sexual nomenclature
That someone else invented. Just ourselves,
That's all we need. We have a spiritual nature

As well as a roast-beef side, and we create
Whatever we might need. Come on, it's late.

SAN JUAN CAPISTRANO DROWNING

Behest: I'm here at your behest, dear Nan,
Hobnobbing with you now as your green spouse,
Your hubcap hubby, hustle-proof old man,
Your goof, your gift, your fool around the house,

Your pliable monster and your mate for life,
Lucky in love this time, your permanent guest
Anchored like iron in the concrete strife
Of love. You're stuck with me: at your behest

I came and stayed and strayed not once; no fox
Am I for sneaking, so you're stuck with me
Till Capistrano's brown adobe walks
Down to the beach and jumps into the sea

And with a ponderous stroke goes swimming west
And stops and sinks and drowns at our behest.

ALMOND ROCA

I have some Almond Roca in my vest,
Wrapped in gold foil and made by Brown and Haley,
Tasty and rich upon the tongue, the best
And sweet (almost) as what you show me daily.

Candy and making love are similar things:
Tasty exteriors, tastier in the middle,
Relished while being had, a feast of kings
For just a little while and always a little

Saddening when the "jump for joy" is over
And all the golden foil is tossed aside
And all that's left are the white sheets of Dover.
Ah, let us move beyond, and let us hide

Our lust this night to talk of loftier things:
Spirits of love and tunes and thoughts with wings.

AT THE BIG SHINDIG CALLED LIFE

There was some laughter, Nan; I heard it not.
Some drinking happened there, and I was found
With an empty glass. A hundred dandies brought
Musical instruments of every sound,

And yet I failed to hear a single note.
Nor did I grab a woman and start to dance,
And no girl said a thing that I could quote,
For no one spoke. I never had a chance.

I never had a chance to break the ice
That never formed and never did arrive;
I tried to think: my thoughts were neither nice
Nor nasty. Was I dead or still alive?

"A little of both, perhaps," declared my Nan,
Steering me clear of flame and frying pan.

YOU'RE A HEN

If I'm a rooster, Nan, why you're a hen,
Prettiest in the barnyard and the smartest,
By far, by far; and five will get you ten,
You'll make this old Rhode Island Red an artist

Tonight before the dark is done. Your face,
It makes me walk on air; you come from Worcester
And have a Boston accent; you wear lace
Elegant now as anything this rooster

Has seen, has seen. And in his barnyard struts
Around the muddy arena he calls home,
His eyes and heart and mind and soul he shuts
To all the hens who wish to borrow his comb.

His eyes want thee, they want no other view:
Please let him cock-a-doodle-doo for you!

FISHING FOR COMPLIMENTS

Fishing for compliments in troubled waters,
I asked my friends and enemies what they thought
Of Nan, my take-home bride. My enemies' daughters
Felt threatened by the things that they had not,

And, muttering, skulked away. My oldest foe,
He tried to charm my Nan with gigolo eyes
And words and winks and handshakes made of dough,
But all he got was knowledge that her thighs

Are true. I turned then to my friends, who stood
Around my Donegal wife to get a look:
All of us stood like statues carved from wood
And none said anything. And then Nan took

The lead and smiled the way a river bends,
And suddenly all those strangers were her friends.

RETURN TO OPPENHEIMER PARK

I needed to get to Oppenheimer Park;
I hadn't been there for a barrel of years;
I knew I had to go there after dark,
Though I could hardly see through all my tears.

In Oppenheimer Park I heard no laughter
At any time in my life; I saw no joy,
No savoring things that I was striving after,
After I won those things. I was a boy

When I first saw the park, my sullen father
Standing behind and cursing under his breath.
There were no other children. Who would bother
To bring the children here? There's rain and death

Throughout the park tonight. The morning brings
Only the silence and the empty swings.

TO A SENIOR LADY

Let's spend old age together, elegant lady,
 Strolling into the sunset hand in hand;
I've got some health insurance and a weighty
 Annuity to share, and you've got land.

We'll build colonial dreams as we grow older,
 Until we dream no more. I'm sixty-five,
And just the other night, upon my shoulder,
 I thought I felt a hand that wasn't alive.

Lightly it tapped me several times: I thought
 I heard a silent voice that said, "You'll go
Sooner than that; the woman, she will not.
Don't wait and waste." Oh lady, let me know

 This very night what only heaven knows
 And help me find my angle of repose.

I CAUGHT AN OCTOPUS

I caught an octopus, a small one, once,
While fishing off the docks in Puget Sound:
"What are you doing on my hook, you dunce?"
I said, as all his tentacles flailed around

And thrashed and broke the surface with a fury.
"I'm trying to fish," I said, "for cod and flounder,
Not some red rubbery freak. I'm in a hurry,
So please get off my hook. A Puget Sounder

Like me has more important things to do."
But here the little octopus looked at me
With his sad eyes and said, "The trouble with you
And all your kind is that you think the sea

Owes you a life. You're wrong. It owes you none
—Though you will cut these legs off, one by one."

NAN'S MAGICIAN

Special occasions call for special effects,
So let me make some moodless magic for you:
I'll make things disappear: some birds, some decks
Of cards, some scarves, some cotton (how I adore you),

Some rings and clean white rabbits; all will go
Into thin air as soon as I snap my fingers,
And I'll be much applauded for my show.
I'll bow and exit . . . . Ah, but something lingers:

The things I wanted to vanish are still here:
My pettiness, my moods, my holding sway
With fatuous talk, my failure to be near
At times, at times. I'll make these go away

And hide their faces in some distant land,
My love, if you will teach me sleight-of-hand.

OUIJA BOARD

We held the Ouija board upon our knees
And faced each other in my dusty room,
Teacher and student letting our fingers tease
The pale planchette's suggestions into bloom.

We got a couple of answers from young Kevin,
Who was the spirit living under the board.
He died in Eire in eighteen-fifty-seven,
Depressed by all the hearts he couldn't afford.

I couldn't help it: half way through the game
I leaned and kissed your adolescent face,
And you responded sweetly, without shame.
Well, that was thirty years ago. In case

You have forgotten, it was I whose knees
Were touching yours that day and saying Please.

ON THE MONTLAKE BRIDGE
IN SEATTLE

Driving across the Montlake Bridge at five,
Alone in traffic, listening to the news:
They say an elderly man was found alive
Under a building that collapsed. I use

This item to recall the things I did
That fell on me last year. On this high span
My tires make a hum on the metal grid
While boats pass underneath. A single man,

I tell myself, can't hold his world together
Without the help of something he is not;
Without that comfort, he becomes a feather
That's whirling in the wind and can't be caught.

And can't be caught? I'm crossing Montlake Bridge.
I've got a couple of six-packs in the fridge.

LOVE IN THE SUPERMARKET

Sometimes I see us in the supermarket
In sundry dreams: we push our shopping cart
Into the produce section, where we park it
By carrots as we listen to the heart

We seem to share between us; then we go
To look at meats and hug in front of bacon
And sausages. We see someone we know
—Who cares, who cares? So what if we are taken

Quite by surprise as we are kissing near
The laundry soaps or by the kitchen wares
Or rolling on the floor beside the beer
Or breaking jars of mustard? Now who cares?

Damn it, it's just a dream, an idle dream.
Then we awake, and things are as they seem.

SHE STILL LOOKS GREAT

I first met Betty on or around a plane
(I'm not sure which) a number of years ago
(I don't recall how many) —sounds insane,
But I don't know just where we said hello

For the first time —it could have been Bombay,
Or Minsk, for all I know; in any case
We didn't meet again until we were gray
And getting long in tooth. Her pretty face,

It's all still there, so delicate and fine
(This sounds like flattery but it's not). It's clear
She's gained in beauty; every delicate line
Bespeaks her gentleness. I hold her dear.

Oh, yes (and wouldn't you know it), she likes cats,
As I do too, and we're both democrats!

LIZZIE BORDEN

I thought of Lizzie Borden all day long,
A masculine-looking woman who'd wear slacks
If she were living today, and sing a song
Like "Slaughter on Tenth Avenue." The axe?

Well, what about the axe? And did she do it?
We heard she took a piece of oak one time
And propped it high and then proceeded too hew it
Into a million pieces, making a chime

Each time she missed and hit the flagstone floor.
"God damn," she'd say, "God damn," again and again,
Sweating and burning to her very core,
"God damn the way they lie. I have no sin

Unless it's trying to love where love must crawl
Upon its belly in a father's hall."

TO A TRUCK DRIVER I MET IN LITTLE AMERICA, WYOMING

Looks like you don't put Levis in the dryer
But rather hang them out-of-doors to dry,
To make them fresh and stiff and snug —attire
For one like you who wears a black string tie

That's held with Navajo silver. Should I chuckle
When looking at your hand-tooled belt that shows
A heifer kicking bulls, your big brass buckle
With Kenworth emblem, your lean cowboy pose

That's rounded out with Stetson, Justin boots,
And crimson shirt with a dozen pearly snaps?
You know I will not chuckle in cahoots
With other Chauvinists, my friend. Perhaps

Some day you'll be my woman, my Queen Mab.
Go now, my sweet, and mount into the cab.

I DIED FOR SUBJECT MATTER

I died for subject matter, and you died
For style. They buried us in Kansas City
Under a fireplug. At first I cried,
While you were doing your nails. Ah, very pretty!

I don't remember what we talked about
The first millennium, but by the second
Your nails had dried, and we had figured out
That everything is style —or so we reckoned,

Thinking that subject matter never existed
But rather took the form of something gone
Before the game began. And then we listed
Our reasons for our answers. Time went on.

What shall we have for dinner, love? —thin air?
I love your nails. What happened to your hair?

A CERTAIN FEAR

I fear, I fear for my, I fear for my
Untutored heart when you and I are talking
Over a cup of chocolate and the sky
Is washing streets with rain. Or when we're walking

In winter sunshine 'round the icy lake,
Mentally arm in arm, if not in fact:
I fear for what I make and fail to make
As pictures in my mind when I enact

The scenes I'd like so see you in and can't.
I fear the freedoms in my mind. They're new.
Afraid of my thoughts, I simply can't recant
Because I love the fear. And that's the clue:

To fear, one has to hope and care a lot
And think of losing everything he's got.

HORSES IN THE SURF

I saw some horses frolicking in the surf,
Some huge white horses frolicking in the spray;
Turning sure-footed as though they ran on turf
Instead of sand. I saw some children play

Just south of where the horses were. They made
Three castles and a dam of sand, and then
They knocked them down. The horses neighed
And galloped, turning sharply, as though men

Were riding them, although they gave no rides.
Later the children rose and ran for home,
Abandoning the ruins to the tides
That slowly smoothed the sand as with a comb.

After a while the horses stopped and stood,
Dead in the water, statues made of wood.

IF THERE'S HELL

If there's a hell, that's where I'm going, Nancy;
Dark are my thoughts and cankerous are my deeds;
If there's a paradise it's more than chancy
That I'm the sort of heel that heaven needs.

And as for you, you're going to where the good
Must always go, the place that has no blame;
It's just a kind of tranquil neighborhood
With music, grass, and trees that have no name.

You live in heaven whether alive or dead:
A woman like yourself with positive heart
That seldom needs a table or a bed
Shall live in grace and harmony and art.

Can I come visit you some sunny day?
I only live a couple of blocks away.

GOOD FRIDAY, DRIVING WESTWARD

I had a nightmare recently: a man
Was being crucified in my hometown
As I was driving westward in my van
With all my worldly goods, to seek renown.

The fellow was upside down upon the cross
And blood was seeping where the nails went through;
The town was all in mourning over the loss
Of such a model citizen as you.

You were my father once, but then you moved
Away and lived with Madeleine under her roof.
You stayed too long. The only thing you proved
Was that the act of hatred needs no proof.

I drove all night, and when the heavens parted,
I was alive and right back where I started.

AN AGED GOLFER'S BUT A PALTRY THING

The ball: where is it now? Oh yes, it lies
Upon the green, right where it landed. Yes,
I had forgotten. Yes. Sometimes my eyes
Deceive my mind. Sometimes I make a mess.

The nine-iron's fine for going high, but not
For rolling things across the green. That takes
The you-know-what-I-mean —I ought to jot
Some more of these things down. I have some snakes

Inside my brains, slowly eating their fill.
They'll take me all away before they're through.
I'll play some golf before they have their will,
And you will wonder where I went, and you

Will know me but I won't know you, dear heart,
And we'll be here and continents apart.

A TRIBUTE TO HORACE

Chatty, sophisticated, modest, sane,
Disarming, witty, natty, charismatic,
Courteous, gracious, polite, and so urbane,
Well-mannered, unromantic, sly, emphatic,

Indifferent, generous, suave, inventive, deft,
Relaxed, dynamic, versatile, sardonic,
Sweet, perspicacious, rallying, moot, bereft
Of clumsiness, ingenuous, ironic,

Tart, introvertish, extrovertish, loose,
Aristocratic, rhythmic, loyal, oblique,
Inspired, self-reliant, never obtuse,
Rare, worldly, precious, Spartan, and unique,

Unwavering, philosophical, well-read,
Immortal, cosmic, reified —and dead!

SHE KNEW CLARK GABLE

I saw an old-time actress at the stable,
Putting her horse up after riding hard.
I knew she acted once with Mr. Gable,
Playing a scene in which he stabbed a guard

Then rode away, away, away. I said,
I wonder if you'd tell me how it was,
Working with such a man, now that he's dead
These forty years. The actress said, "How does

A person even begin? When he was young
He had a thousand one-night stands, I'll bet;
I hated kissing him because his tongue
Was casual and his breath was bad. And yet

He was a temperate man and saw no red,
Saddled his horse and never lost his head."

THE FURBELOW

Balanced my checkbook late this morning, paid
Some bills, and dusted some around the house,
    Which needed it again. And then I made
A sandwich. I no longer have a spouse.

    And that's all right, if one gets underway
And doesn't let his ship stand still at anchor.
      I think of her occasionally in the day
And even less at night. I ought to thank her

    For cutting me loose a couple of years ago
And teaching me that what I thought I wanted
      Was insubstantial as a furbelow
Attached to one by whom the house is haunted.

    Oh, I'm aware that Julia is still here,
If only as a ghost, so far and near.

THE FULL PROFESSORS

Some of the full professors published books,
Some of them published nothing, while the others
Wrote poems about the way a pansy looks
And talked about the damage from their mothers.

All lived the mental life, or so they thought
(They parked their brains behind their alma maters);
They faced their classes but they seldom taught,
Except when eyeing one another's daughters.

Some of the full professors worked like ants,
Some of them stepped on ants, and some played pool
All day, some had affairs, some wet their pants,
Some quit, some died. And one of them was a fool

Who spoke the facts. This was Professor Brown,
The village imbecile, the campus clown.

PLEASE LEAVE THE SEAT UP

Please leave the seat up so the cat can drink,
After you've gone to Mexico with Fred.
I should be home in a couple of days, I think,
To tidy up. So please don't make the bed.

Besides, I'd like to see the pecker-tracks
The bastard leaves, so I can visualize
The way you two make one. I'll bet he smacks
You right across the buns to energize

Your hips. You squeeze him like a pair of pliers;
He pulls his rusty nail out of the wood
And pounds it in again. He lights your fires
And you light his. There goes the neighborhood.

Oh, by the way, you need not feed the cat.
He's quick as light, and he can catch a rat.

EZEKIEL CALLED

Ezekiel called the other day: he said
He wanted to talk to You about the meeting,
And whether or not to summon up the dead
And ask them to attend. There's been some cheating,

He said, on those exams at Heaven's gate,
And some were getting in who ought to fall.
I told him You'd agree but You'd be late
In getting to the meeting, if at all.

I took the liberty of telling him
Your secret policy, and how it's based
On flattery and on mythological whim.
I told him how You said that in Your haste

You got the whole thing inexcusably wrong.
I told him how it bored You, all along.

DESIRE AND OLD AGE

Ecstasy's hard to find in sunset years,
And bliss is just as scarce, it seems to me;
And as for genuine love, the old man fears
The nectar of the stress would kill the bee.

What's one to do, then? Put away the plow?
Forget the sensual furrows of one's youth?
Live only for the "then" and not the "now"?
Be bored to tears by telling just the truth?

No, that's too easy. Better to take a walk
Right down the middle of the Interstate
And let the angry autos swerve and squawk
With truculent horns, than merely vegetate.

Better to exit now, and better dead
Than longing for the longing that has fled.

DOWN IN COLORADO SPRINGS

And when you get to Colorado Springs,
I hope Pike's Peak is standing guard for you,
Bright in the April air, with lazy rings
Of light around it, pale Picasso blue.

For you, I hope the Academy inspires
(Its architecture saying "I like Ike"),
With keen-as-cutlery cathedral spires
Pale as the pewter in a Jan Van Eyck.

For you, I hope the Broadmoor's old and fine,
As it's cracked up to be, with six retired
Generals in the lobby, after Holbein,
Remembering all the wars their anger sired.

I hope you're into politics and things;
The wind blows hard in Colorado Springs.

PEGASUS HOUSE

Pegasus House: please take me there when all
My scurrying days are done and I am filled
With loathing for the world and long to fall
And not get up. Please take me there! I've willed

The words that make this poem to those I love
And all the space between these lines to those
I'd love to see below. Lift me above
And let me live in that winged house and close

These soot-black days. And when in Pegasus House
I'll look for friends and find a few and maybe
An enemy here and there, but mostly douse
My sorrows with ale. And if I love you, baby,

Just take this axe, cut off the horse's head,
And place it under the covers in my bed.

THANKSGIVING WITHOUT MARY M.

I spent Thanksgiving all alone. I sat
In front of the television, watching games,
Sharing a TV dinner with the cat,
And trying to recall your lovers' names.

Christmas was even worse. I had the 'flu,
And being sick alone is doubly sad,
Or triple with the loss of lovely you
And all the tricks you played to make me glad.

Easter is here, but please don't bother to rise,
I tell myself. Stay off your tired legs.
She isn't coming back. She's closed her eyes
And gone to look for heavenly Easter eggs.

Bedtime again. The sleeplessness that kills
By killing not. I take a couple of pills.

LOST LOVE, 1961

Dearly beloved, we are gathered here
To pay our last respects to stupid thoughts:
' One was the thought that you and I could steer
A steady course through stiff forget-me-nots

That lay across our path; another one,
More frivolous than the first, was that our lot
Would be a dreamer's world with nothing but sun
And shoeshine tunes. Ah, but the silliest thought

Of all was that I'd always honor you
And never stray and never fall below
The Emersonian standard that we knew.
I let you down. I failed. I stubbed my toe.

And now you're gone and I am in my chair
Reading of Walden Pond and trying to care.

THE DEADBOLT

I put a deadbolt on my heart. I chained
My fellow-feelings in a basement bin;
I took what little sympathy remained
And flushed it down the toilet. Please come in,

I said, although I wished you gone. Please come
And tell me what's been happening to us,
What's wrong with our pale blood, and why we're dumb
And speechless as a crowd upon a bus.

And so we argued all the afternoon
And settled nothing. Utterly we failed.
You put my heart upon a tablespoon
And bent it back and flipped it. Then I nailed

Our hands together. They heard us up above,
Talking our heads off, never mentioning love.

THE POET CUBE

I keep a five-inch cube upon my desk,
With a picture of a poet on each side.
For instance, when I'm waxing Whitmanesque,
I turn the cube so Walt can be my guide.

And when I'm feeling countrified or lost,
I move my cube a quarter-turn and find
The wrinkled countenance of Robert Frost.
This never works. I merely fall behind.

Sometimes I turn the thing to Robert Bly,
In hopes that Iron John will pull me out
Of writer's block. There's something in my eye;
I think it's fustian; I am passing out.

I turn then to the last side, look and see:
My God, is this a photograph of me?

THE ESSENCE OF COMEDY

I watched an old Jack Benny show on cable,
A blend of understatement and some miming,
Some quizzical face-expressions and an able
Supporting cast, and almost perfect timing.

Outside, the moon was sidling out of a cloud
And rising full, like bread with plenty of yeast,
And slippery-looking too. There was a crowd
Of critics trying to climb the moon. A beast

Was chasing them and looking quite annoyed.
George Meredith was there, and Bergson too,
Charles Lamb, Bill Hazlitt, and a Doctor Freud,
With old museum theories out of the blue.

The moon, it kept on climbing into the night.
It looked so empty and it looked so right.

THE PITCHFORK FARMER GIVES DIRECTIONS

To get to Clementville, you take a right
At Johnson's Corner, by the rhubarb fields
—Or maybe that's alfalfa —there's a bright
Red barn right by the crossroads there that shields

The little house behind it from the sun
(That's where the Klemmer folks were murdered back
In 'fifty-three by robbers on the run).
Well, anyhow, you'll see a broken shack

After you've gone eleven miles, on the left;
And on the side of the shack there is a sign
That says: "If you lived here you'd be bereft
Of love and hope and be no friend of mine."

The road gets wider there for just a spell,
And then dead-ends. That's Clementville. That's Hell.

OLD ORVILLE TO HIS WIFE
ON THEIR FIFTIETH

I think I'd like to end this in a while;
We're oil and water now; we just don't mix;
I'm viscous oil, the kind that stretches a mile
When tankers leak and sea birds sink like bricks.

And you, you're water, pure as pumps can give
When hooked by silver pipes to magical springs
Where birds might dip their beaks and sing and live
Their rancid lives by telling lies. These rings

We gave each other fifty years ago
Are heavy now and seem like lead or zinc,
The leaves are dead, the sunshine's under snow,
My body's numb, I neither feel nor think.

It's hard for me to love you in this weather,
Now that our spotted skins have turned to leather.

IN CAHOOTS

Cahoots is what we're in when we're in love,
Conspiring to uphold the physical code,
The one that's scoffed at by the turtle dove
That rides the air that Casanova rode.

Cahoots is what we're in when we have sex,
Conspiring hard to hold our thighs together
Until our ship of groans finally wrecks
Upon the rocks that slide beneath this weather.

Lothario's not my name, and yours is neither
Calypso, Scarlett O., nor Jezebel.
Yet we are flesh and folk, and we will either
Make love or die. And those can go to hell

Who think that life is serious. It is not.
Cahoots is all it was and all we've got.

NIGHTMARES

Bumper-to-bumper traffic in my brains
All through the night, one bad dream after another:
First I was falling, then I was in chains,
And then I was rejected by my mother.

She held a cattle-prod and poked me here
And there, and tried to hold my tiny hand
Under the scalding water. How could I fear
The most angelic person in the land?

Then I awoke all twisted in the sheet
And sweating like a man about to hang;
Anger and guilt were wrapped around my feet
Like shackles on a hopeless Georgia gang.

My mother died some thirty years ago
—And still she holds me gently by the toe.

THE BULLY OUT OF THE PAST

At Denver International Airport: how
I recognized him after all those years
Had more to do with what we will allow
Ourselves to be in pain about than tears

That fell upon a playground during the war,
The Hitler war: he was the one who knocked
My knees away and held me down and swore
He'd cut off both my thumbs. My parents were shocked

Of course, but shrugged and told me to "abide."
I knew the bully knew me by the way
His eyes touched mine and quickly snapped aside
As he went limping by, so weak and gray.

I had a suitcase made by Samsonite;
I looked down at my knuckles: they were white.

THE BOX-KITE (AFTER TALKING WITH A YOUNG WOMAN)

High as a big box-kite I drove away
In spirits elevated by her smiles;
I danced upon a string, and I held sway
Against the clouds in hot Chicago styles.

I knew this couldn't last, this buzz she gave me
With coffee conversations half the day;
Her pale red hair and her attempts to save me
Were all that I remembered on my way

To my bleak rooms. When I was half way home,
The gale began to slow, and my brave kite
Wobbled and fell. And I thought, when in Rome
Do what you will. And so, with all my might,

I yanked the string and broke it in my mind,
Leaving the rattling paper far behind.

RAKE UP THE LEAVES

Rake up the leaves, but leave a few for me:
I need to turn them into fantasy-boats
With cobweb sails to sail the fishpond sea
With love and heart and everything that floats.

Let me pretend that I am at the helm
Of the first ship that enters your dark bay;
Let me pretend that I shall overwhelm
Your nautical heart with all that admirals say.

Fantasy is the wind that makes me move
In my red ships. And love is what you'll find
Deep in my cargo holds, where I shall prove
That I am yours in flesh and soul and mind.

Rake up the leaves, and leave your love for me,
In pantries of the heart where you shall be.

BOTTICELLI'S SECRET WISH

I talked with Botticelli in a dream
Under Uffizi's wall. The painter said,
"I wandered toward the middle of the stream
In every revolution that I led;

"I played it safe with Judith, Flora, Venus
—All of them look like housewives being bored.
I'll tell you something (let's keep this between us):
I'd rather paint a boxer being floored.

"I wish I'd lived in your time, painting Tunney
Losing to Dempsey; Ali (Cassius Clay)
Decking them all and raking in the money,
Carmen Basilio battering Sugar Ray."

Then Botticcelli walked into the shade:
Under Uffizi's wall I saw him fade.

IN ANOTHER COUNTRY (FOR CELIA)

After the funeral in L.A. I caught
A flight back to Seattle. I miss her now
But might not later on. One time I thought
We might grow serious, and I thought of how

We might construct a life, complete with kids
And house and sex and talk and paying bills.
But then the morning light: it often rids
High-flying minds of hopes and levels the hills

The way a 'dozer does when men are building
A house that looks like other houses —fenced,
Festooned with shrubs and stuff. There's no sense gilding
The starkness of the thing that never commenced.

And now she's dead. Apparently she'll be missed;
But then again, we never even kissed.

FLYING ALONG (FOR NAN)

Flying along in a seven fifty-seven,
I wish I were a California man;
At thirty thousand feet I'm close to heaven
But not so close as when I'm close to Nan.

The California landscape slips away,
And then the captain says, "There's Crater Lake,
There on the right-hand side." Who cares, I say;
I've got a crater in my heart; I ache

More than I thought I would, and I will curl
Myself around my pillow late tonight,
And I'll pretend to hold that quotable girl
Who lives so far away and feels so right.

Cynics may say that love is just a myth:
They don't know me; they don't know Nathalie Smith.

THREE-DIMENSIONAL WOMAN

Nan is my love, my three-dimensional girl:
She pleasures me in body, spirit, and mind;
Nan is the wind that makes my flags unfurl
And whip and snap with life; she makes me find

The means to place the means before the ends
And end those lassitudes that pulled me down
During those years of bachelorhood, when friends
Would laugh behind my back and call me clown.

Back then I was as salient as a bird
That's lost its wings and doesn't even know it;
Back in those days I thought I knew the word
And merely couldn't think of how to show it.

Then three-dimensional Nan showed me the source:
"The word is Love," she said. "Of course, of course!"

FANTASIZING NEAR BERKELEY SQUARE

At bay, at bay, at bay, I held my senses
When I first spotted Nan near Berkeley Square,
Working in some dark bookstore: then the fences
Of self-control just barely held me square.

I loved her right away; I fantasized,
Quickly undressing her behind the counter;
I made her work while naked, and I sized
Her breasts and buttocks as I started to mount her.

I bought a copy of "Women in Love" from Nan,
And as she wrapped it I pretended we
Were loving on the counter while the man
Who owned the store was throwing things at me,

Waving his arms and shouting at the top
Of his tobacco lungs: "Don't stop! Don't stop!"

I HEARD A WINDOW BREAK

I heard a window break one night, and quick
I went below to see what I had heard.
Lying in shards of glass I found a brick
With paper wrapped around it. Like a bird

My heart was flying around. I read the note.
It said, "I love you and I need to feel;
You don't know me but I know you. I dote
Upon your body and soul, and I would kneel

In public places to perform such acts
As people are arrested for." I spent
A week or so in wondering what the facts
Behind it were. I never knew. I went

About my business, busier by the day,
Until the crazy wondering went away.

TO A WELL-BUILT WOMAN

I wonder what you're doing today, my friend,
  My irrefragable torso. Are you reading
Some "War and Peace" that never seems to end?
  Or are you finding war within and needing

A hug from me to help you through the task?
  Maybe you're still in bed and having visions
  In which I answer everything you ask,
  Except about the bruises and incisions.

Perhaps you're being assertive now and striding
  To fetch the dueling pistols from the case.
I hope you shoot me dead as we are riding
  On one another. I hope I see your face

Precisely at the moment of your bliss,
When urgent voices say: Oh this! Oh this!

WASHING OUR CLOTHES TOGETHER

Symbolically I do our laundry, Nancy,
Bright blouses, shirts and skirts, and underwear;
It's easy with machines, but I am antsy
Whenever I mix these colors dark and fair.

Right on the garments' labels I am told,
"Wash with similar colors." Disregard,
My heart is telling me. Though I am old,
I want to wash with you. Should that be hard?

What's life, if not the mixing of those things
That never should be mixed, and what is death,
If not the separating of our wings
From our cold brains, my love? So with this breath,

I start the process that will make us clean,
And blue and red and orange and yellow and green.

OLD AGE DEFIANCE

When friends are few and old and far between;
When there's a vegetation at our knees
That seeks to cover us; when we have seen
Dead lands beyond the psyche's seven seas;

When pains that should be aches distract our souls
And hold us from the business of the day;
When we're more interested in digging holes
Than building happy lamps to light the way:

Then we should take a look around and take
An inventory of the things we fear;
And we should seize these fustian things and break
Them over our knees and shout for all to hear:

Hey! It's too soon to throw us in the ditch;
Hey! We're not ready yet, you son of a bitch!

IGNORING VALENTINE'S DAY

Valentine's Day is something I ignore,
Except when something special haunts my thought;
Then all my thoughts go marching through the door
And head straight for your house. And like as not,

I'll lie awake tonight, holding your face
Against my own, if only in my brain;
And since the imagination is the place
To do whatever we want in sun or rain,

I shall entwine with you and drink your breath
Throughout the night; I'll feel your body curl
Against my chest and legs. There is no death
So long as love can find the boy and girl

Who hid so long ago beneath our hair
When we were green and strong, and all was fair.

POLISHING WITH FRANK SINATRA

Listening to Frank Sinatra sing a medley
Of optimum songs, I wax my car again;
A Sunday afternoon is pretty deadly
When they are gone away and now is then.

A man who's twice divorced has got to show
That he's not putting on a show; he must
Become a distance runner: stop-and-go
And stop-and-go can't win the viscera's trust.

I smear the Simonize around, then buff
The Chrysler with my buffing glove. I drive
Around the lake again. That off-the-cuff
Approach of old Sinatra —man alive!

I lost my Ava too, I say to Frank;
I don't know whom to blame and whom to thank.

UNWED PREGNANT TEENAGER

Now there's a brat within a brat: the tart
Carries her future welfare checks inside
Her belly as she rolls her Safeway cart
Across the sticky lot. She's full of pride

With how important she will be quite soon
When seven doctors and ten social workers
Jump through her hoops to sing her selfish tune,
For which we pay. A generation of shirkers

Descends upon us, whining loud and smothering
Whatever honor's left. Needless to say,
The father's gone and she will do the mothering
Catch as catch-can. I watch her walk and sway

With ponderous pregnant step, like someone old.
It makes me angry that she's carrying gold.

THE SURGE OF LOVE

It catches me off guard —the surge, I mean,
The one that hits me in the throat so hard
When you appear in dresses red or green
Or any hue —it catches me off guard.

It's not your beauty only, it's your way
Of suddenly being there, as if you came
Out of a wall that stands between the day
And measly night. Nathalie, you're the flame

That drives me from my would-be cozy coffin.
Living is being taken by surprise
More often than we like but not as often
As we might need, to keep from being wise.

Being alive is being caught off guard,
Tripping on ropes of love and falling hard.

SOME GEESE WERE STROLLING

Some geese were strolling south of Capitol Lake,
As we were strolling north. I said to them,
   "How do you like this lady that I take
For walks each day? Now isn't she a gem?"

They didn't answer me. They walked on past,
Swaying from side to side, with heads held high.
   It didn't matter; nothing mattered at last:
I had my Nathalie with me, and the sky.

The overcast was low, like ponderous quilts
That covered over our bodies as we walked.
   I felt like one upon a pair of stilts
Whenever Nathalie smiled at me and talked.

A man on stilts is one who's high, I guess;
You should have seen her in that taffeta dress.

CRIMSON OLDSMOBILE

I saw my son today. He waved at me
As he drove by in a crimson Oldsmobile.
He didn't look. He simply waved at me
Then slid around the corner like an eel.

I'm glad I had my glimpse. I'm glad he had
Whatever he had to have to be as cruel
As one must be to break away —the sad
But necessary stuff of after-school.

Good luck, my son! I hope you drive your Olds
A couple o' billion miles around the stars;
I hope you find, before the evening folds,
What you are looking for in angry bars.

And if you go to heaven, I hope you'll wave
To me as you go by —so sad, so brave.

THE OLD SCHOLAR IS LOSING IT

Son of a bitch, I say, God damn it all,
Can't find my dictionary or my pipe,
Can't find my itchy novel by Stendhal,
Can't find my reading glasses or the ripe

Tomato that was sitting on my desk.
Can't find the God-damn notes that I was taking
To write an article on the arabesque,
Can't find my room, and sometimes I'm mistaking

My house for someone else's, and our town
For cities elsewhere. Oh, sometimes the nation's
A country I can't find. I'm drifting down,
Light in the head and full of warm sensations

That make me feel much less than what I am.
Son of a bitch, I say. I say God damn.

DIRTY VIDEO

I watched a dirty video late last night,
Lying in bed with telephone off the hook
And drink in hand. You know, it's quite a sight,
A woman lying there and reading a book

With two guys doing God knows what to her.
It didn't arouse me, though; my mood was down
And you'd been gone a couple of weeks. Abjure
All thoughts of her, I told myself, and drown

Your sorrows in this irrepressible smut;
She isn't coming back. The Cliffs of Dover
Will walk to France before she comes, so shut
Your mind and watch the show until it's over.

Just let it sink and sing the Rock of Ages
While this brave woman shrieks and turns the pages.

NANTUCKET ISLAND

Nantucket is a green and silvery place,
Shaped like a bent triangle, with curt trees,
Expensive sand, and many a weathered face
On house and human alike. If you say "Please,"

The merchants will address you smooth as honey,
Provided you buy the sweatshirt and the poster
That shows the widow's walks and how old money
Had bent the streets. You never hear a boaster

—Nantucket is above that kind of thing;
The theme you hear runs quietly in the mind,
And always leaves an ancient hint of a sting,
Like salty winds —a meaning we can't find.

Beauty has special sadnesses, I'm told:
Do you feel lonely now? Do you feel old?

THE MINEFIELD

There is a minefield here, from days of war,
Which never has been cleared; it is a green
And dangerous place to walk. It flings the gore
Of citizens now and then, who last were seen

Venturing on the innocent-looking grass.
Love is a minefield, too, it seems to me:
We have to watch just where we step and pass
The tests of luck, to reach the place where we

Are safe. Shall we go hand in hand today?
Together we can figure where to walk,
What to avoid, and what to ask and say.
And will we blow sky-high, and will this chalk

Be used to mark the outlines of our parts,
Our arms and legs, and our aluminum hearts?

THE PRIMORDIAL
LOCOMOTIVE

Curt and abrupt the weather was today:
The thunder spoke but briefly, and the rain
Was quick to strike our faces as we lay
Across the tracks and waited for the train.

We felt it in the ground before we heard it;
We heard the crossing signals start to clang;
And then we heard the whistle. We preferred it
To be as quick as possible. You sang

A kind of dirge, and I told you to hurry
—The tall black train was breathing down our necks
And soon to cut those necks in two. "Don't worry,"
You said, "Don't worry, Darling, this is sex,

And this is climax-time. There is no train.
The thing that shakes the land is in your brain."

DARK THOUGHTS AT THE SKOKOMISH RIVER

The waters are so high they almost touch
The underside of the bridge I'm standing on.
The dark carousing currents are too much
For anything in their path. Before the dawn

The bridge will fall; it trembles even now,
Beneath my feet, and I can feel the planks
Starting to shift. The man-made must kowtow
To nature's demon moods. The river's banks

Are helpless parents with a maniac child
Who throws his toys around: houses and trees
Go swirling down, and more debris is piled
Against my bridge. It cannot hold. My knees

Are ready to be shattered in the kill;
My heart is ready to dry upon the hill.

WHAT A NICE FIGURE YOU HAVE!

We're multi-lingual, are we not? You speak
In English at the moment, but at times
You speak in body language too. I seek
To understand this more. I hear the chimes

Inside my skull whenever you cross your legs
And lean a little, just to make your point,
With outstretched fingers, like some lovely pegs
On which to hang my thoughts. I disappoint

Myself whenever you move, because it's not
To be —and yet I seek to watch you move.
Keep disappointing me! It's such a thought
That even its denial seems to prove

That here and there we find a crimson rose
That can't be plucked. And everybody knows.

THE TIME YOU BEHEADED ME

I hadn't been beheaded for a while,
In metaphor, that is, until you snapped
My neck in two for causing you to smile
While I was joking about the handicapped.

Here's my defense: we *all* are handicapped
By being human; every joke is sick
When nothing in the world is well. You slap
My arrogant face now, and you try to kick

My shins, my knees, my private parts. I hold
Your flailing wrists and nip you on the neck.
We fall upon the bed then. We are bold.
We try the ten positions. Thus we check

Our innocence by the door that leads to hell,
By getting sick and then by getting well.

THE COUPLE IN THE NIGHT CAFE

"Let's just be friends," she said; "let's just be friends."
"Where have I heard that line before," I said.
"Platonic is the best," she said; "no ends
And no beginnings. Love is never dead

When it's restricted to the mind and soul."
I sat in silence then. I ate my chili,
And with my bread I sopped the dark brown bowl.
She ate her greens. The evening's willy-nilly

At best, I thought. I wished that I were home.
But then she smiled at me and asked me up
To her apartment, and she took her comb
And moved it through her hair. My coffee cup

Was quivering in my hand. And were we brave
As we climbed up, to Aristotle's cave?

TOO MANY VICTIMS

Victims are much the fashion in these days;
Lawsuits today are just a way of life;
The one who bumps you by mistake, he pays
Yourself, your kids, your cousins, and your wife.

I heard a story Monday that I sent
To all the sleazy tabloids I could find:
A man filed suit against the excrement
That was his own, for soiling his behind.

The jury found him right, but then the judge
Scolded him up one side and down the other
For stinking up the courtroom with his fudge.
The frivolous man was sent home to his mother,

Who promptly filed a suit against her son
For hurting her in birth. Of course she won.

OLDER MAN IN THE HOSPITAL

The doctor's just a kid, not twenty-seven,
And yet he has a Norman Rockwell manner;
Whether it's time for me to go to heaven
He won't quite say. He'll put me under the scanner

Again to search for things that should not be,
While I lie flat and straight and perfectly still,
Like freight. He says he doesn't expect to see
"Unusual things" (he means the things that kill).

The kindly liar leaves. My body sleeps.
I dream of Norman Rockwell's art: those faces,
So normal that they give a person the creeps,
So full of blood that's out of control in places

Where blood should never be. Of course I'll die.
Cancer's American as apple pie.

WHY I WRITE IN RHYME

Coming out of the woodwork, I observed
Some others coming out of the woodwork too;
I saw that they were poets well preserved
In steep traditions of free verse, and few,

If any, said they ever wrote in rhyme.
One said it was confining, and another
Declared he really didn't have the time
To shape and fit the sounds. One said his mother

Had nearly killed him off when he was three
With nursery rhymes and other mindless chants.
But all of them insisted they were free
By going rhymeless. Here they dropped their pants

To show how free they were. And they ran fast,
Stumbling along with trousers at half-mast.

THE LOST MAN'S CHOICES

For no particular reason, I have lost
The things I beat my brains out to achieve;
For no discernible reason, I have cost
Myself a fortune in what all believe

To be essential: I mean friends and love,
Relationships that span so many years,
The grace I used to have from God above,
And even love of self. I took my fears

And made them into bricks. I built a wall,
A ten-foot wall, to keep my enemies out
And guard my diligent soul. And that is all.
I'll never know what heaven's all about,

And whether sin's in fashion or in season,
Or why we live, for no particular reason.

I STOPPED TO TALK WITH
THIS WOMAN

Are those azaleas, Ma'am? They look like flame
That stopped and froze before it could do harm;
About your dahlias there, they're like the name
Of some young girl I had upon my arm

A thousand years ago and can't remember,
Except to say she stole my brain away.
That blood-red poppy there, it's like the ember
That's keeping me from turning into clay.

You're prettier than your garden, Ma'am, but I
Won't mention it because you'll think, "He means
To take advantage of my restive eye
And touch the rounded denim of my jeans."

I'd be remiss, Ma'am, if I had such thoughts,
Standing among these crude forget-me-nots.

BVG